Uncivil Disobedience

Uncivil Disobedience

STUDIES IN VIOLENCE AND DEMOCRATIC POLITICS

Jennet Kirkpatrick

PRINCETON UNIVERSITY PRESS
PRINCETON AND OXFORD

Published by Princeton University Press, 41 William Street, Princeton, New Jersey 08540

In the United Kingdom: Princeton University Press, 6 Oxford Street, Woodstock, Oxfordshire OX20 1TW

Library of Congress Cataloging-in-Publication Data

Kirkpatrick, Jennet, 1970–
Uncivil disobedience : studies in violence and democratic politics / Jennet Kirkpatrick.
p. cm.
Includes index.
ISBN 978–0–691–13709–4 (hardcover : alk. paper) —
ISBN 978–0–691–13877–0 (pbk. : alk. paper)
1. Political violence—United States. 2. Militia movements—United States.
3. Vigilance committees—United States. 4. Lynching—United States.
5. Antislavery movements—United States. I. Title.
HN90.V5K53 2008
303.6′20973—dc22
2008004057

British Library Cataloging-in-Publication Data is available

This book has been composed in

Printed on acid-free paper. ∞

press.princeton.edu

Printed in the United States of America

1 3 5 7 9 10 8 6 4 2

For S.B.K
and
D.G.K

CONTENTS

ACKNOWLEDGMENTS

THIS BOOK BEGAN WITH a fascination for an overlooked corner of American political thought, and in researching and writing it, I have incurred intellectual debts that cannot be adequately catalogued or expressed here. These are the sorts of obligations, happily, that are best honored over time and best returned in kind.

I wrote the bulk of this book at the Institute for Advanced Study in conditions that can only be described as idyllic. I am grateful to all the faculty and members of the School of Social Science at the Institute for the academic year 2005–2006. The Law and Public Affairs Program at Princeton University provided me with a second intellectual home, and I am thankful to the fellows and participants. I want especially to acknowledge the criticism and comments of Rebecca Bryant, Clarissa Hayward, Liz Magill, Laure Murat, Michael Peletz, Ian Roxborough, Kim Scheppele, Joan Scott, Zrinka Stahuljak, and Tom Sugrue. For our discussions about the law—written and unwritten—while walking in the Institute woods, I am grateful to Marianne Constable.

My conversations with Michael Walzer provided an opportunity for me to reflect on the substance and the process of what I was writing. Many missteps and wrong turns were avoided due to his remarks, which invariably clarified my mind and crystallized my thinking. During the early stages of this book, Benjamin Barber challenged me at every turn with his characteristic zeal and acumen. He asked the hard questions, trusting that I was capable of addressing, if not answering them.

Don Herzog read the entire manuscript twice and has been a wellspring of humor, guidance, and good will, all of which gave me a much-needed sense of perspective. For their comments on various chapters, I owe thanks to Cristina Beltrán, Mark Brown, Mark Button, Mary Gallagher, David Gutterman, Bonnie Honig, Andreas Kalyvas, Mika LaVaque-Manty, Susan Liebell, Jill Locke, Rob Mickey, Davide Panagia, Arlene Saxonhouse, Liz Wingrove, Jim Young, and Linda Zerilli. The advice of Mary Gallagher, Anna Grzymala-Busse, and Andy Markovits during the final stages of this project was indispensable. Thanks too to Natalie Phelps for her research assistance.

For as long as I can remember, Sandra Kirkpatrick and I have had a running conversation about the finer points of grammar, sentence structure, and word choice. She has a faculty for words like no other. I am especially grateful for her editorial counsel on this book.

Though his intellectual interests are in a different field, Dan Silverman has been a steadfast and attentive critic, offering judgment, insight, and support while I struggled to make sense of America's violent history and its place within democratic theory. I benefited more than I can say from his criticisms and companionship. For their patience during the talkative periods as well as the quiet ones, I am grateful to my family.

Uncivil Disobedience

Introduction

WARTS AND ALL

As WITH MOST WARS, the American war on terror has been depicted in simple terms: America, a defender of democracy, is engaged in a battle against foreign terrorists who are "enemies of freedom," as George Bush has put it. American democracy is on one side of this struggle; terrorism is on the other. The problem with this simple depiction is that it ignores America's long history of a homegrown version of terrorism. Militant abolitionists like John Brown, vigilantes on the western frontier, violent labor groups, lynch mobs in the post-Reconstruction South, and violent right-wing organizations like the militia movement were all terrorists by today's standards. What's more, these violent groups were not opposed to democracy. Indeed, democratic ideas nurtured and legitimated their terrorism.

Consider, for instance, this intriguing bit of American history. In 1854 an interracial mob led by a Unitarian minister smashed down the door of the Boston courthouse in order to free Anthony Burns, a fugitive slave. The mob intervened at almost the last possible moment: the following morning Burns would be escorted to the Boston harbor and, in accordance with the Fugitive Slave Act of 1850, returned to slavery in Virginia. Morally opposed to Burns's rendition and the law that sanctioned it, the Boston mob aimed its battering ram at the courthouse door. Climbing over the splintered rubble, several individuals engaged in hand-to-hand combat with a phalanx of guards. The abolitionist mob was repulsed in fairly short order, and its attempt to free Burns was unsuccessful. Though brief, its battle with the legal authorities was intense and deadly. In the melee, a guard was killed.

The killing caused a furor among abolitionists in Boston and beyond. Debate centered on two prominent abolitionists who delivered fiery speeches minutes before the attack on the courthouse. Wendell Phillips, an abolitionist crusader known for his oratorical eloquence, and Theodore Parker, the president of the Boston Vigilance Committee, exhorted their audience of five thousand to act on behalf of liberty rather than only talking about its value and import. Phillips urged his audience to recall that they lived in the revolutionary city of Boston, where, he hoped, "the children of Adams and Hancock may prove that they are not bastards." "Let us prove," he urged, "that we are worthy of liberty." Parker confronted legal obligation to the Fugitive Slave Act and the issue of violence directly. Advising disobedience to slave law, he exhorted his audience to instead follow "the law of the people," which "is in your hands and arms" and can be executed "just when you see fit." Execution of this populist law, Parker suggested, could require drastic measures. There "is a means and there is an end; liberty is the end, and sometimes peace is not the means toward it."[1]

Whatever their immediate effect on the abolitionist audience, Phillips and Parker's speeches proved prophetic. By the 1850s, militant abolitionists were increasingly willing to entertain the idea that, like their revolutionary predecessors, they might have to employ violent means to attain liberty. More abolitionists openly and violently defied the Fugitive Slave Act. By 1856 the violence had escalated: John Brown led a deadly raid on a proslavery settlement in Kansas in which five men were dragged from their cabins and hacked to death on the banks of Pottawatomie Creek. Three years later Brown attacked the federal armory in Harper's Ferry, West Virginia, in a desperate attempt to spark more widespread violent resistance to slavery. Brown was pilloried by some and lauded by others. Thoreau, for instance, compared Brown to Ethan Allen and Cromwell and defended his "perfect right to interfere by force with the slaveholder in order to rescue the slave." His violence was "employed in a righteous cause."[2]

Like the Boston mob, other American groups have become enamored with the idea of righteous violence. They might logically be called "uncivil disobedients"—that is, groups of citizens who, protesting unjust laws or legal actions and upholding established political ideals, commit illegal and violent acts. Uncivil disobedients typically lay claim to many of the same ideals that prompted the American Revolution. They often look at the American revolutionaries with admiration for their idealistic commitment to liberty, their participatory zeal, and their militancy. The citizens who violently protested against the government in the late eighteenth century—in Shays's Rebellion in 1786–87, the Whiskey Rebellion in 1794, and then Fries's Rebellion in 1799—did not, for instance, see themselves as rebels. Rather, they understood their acts as preserving republicanism, guarding liberty, and upholding the ideals of the Declaration of Independence.

Vigilantes have also traditionally justified their violence by appealing to the right of revolution and self-preservation and the ideal of popular sovereignty. The first instance of vigilantism occurred in 1780 when Colonel Charles Lynch, a lapsed Quaker, and a band of leading citizens arrested, tried, and punished Tories plundering property on Virginia's western

[1] Stevens, *Anthony Burns*, 38–39, 293–95.
[2] Thoreau, *Higher Law*, 132–33.

boarder. Offenders received thirty-nine lashes and were required to proclaim "Liberty Forever!" More vigilantes followed. Over two hundred vigilance committees formed on the western frontier, and, in the post-Reconstruction South, lynch mobs claimed nearly three thousand victims. As I write this introduction, a vigilante group called the Minutemen has recently made national headlines as they police the U.S.-Mexico border searching for undocumented immigrants. There's reason to think that this latest resort to vigilantism is not an anomaly. Vigilante themes are prevalent in Hollywood, ranging from the trite and harmless (*Batman*, *Spiderman*) to the violent and vengeful (*Death Wish*, *Falling Down*). Moreover, polling data suggest that a portion of the American population is sympathetic to the idea that vigilantism is sometimes appropriate: a CBS/*New York Times* Monthly Poll found that 31 percent of respondents agreed that there are times when people might need to take the law into their own hands.[3]

As well as cropping up regularly throughout American history, uncivil disobedients have appeared on both ends of the political spectrum. On the left, portions of the labor movement adopted violent methods to improve the lot of working men and women. The results include the terrorism of the Molly Maguires, a group of anthracite coal miners in Pennsylvania that bullied supervisors for better working conditions in the 1860s, the infamous explosion in Haymarket Square in 1886, the violent strikes in Coeur d'Alene and Pullman in the 1890s, and the dynamiting of the *Los Angeles Times* in 1910. The Weather Underground, the Symbionese Liberation Army, and radical environmental and animal rights groups have also claimed the mantle of righteous violence. On the right, Carry Nation and her hymn-singing compatriots in the temperance movement smashed bars and stock with hatchets to protest weakened prohibition laws in Kansas. More recently, violent religious groups have killed those who provide abortions, and the militia movement has advocated violent resistance to a tyrannical and oppressive government. Looked at from the vantage point of the history of righteous violence, American civil society has had a notable uncivil streak.[4]

The Burns affair and this larger history of uncivil disobedience remind us of an ignored relationship between democratic ideas, violence, and terrorism. Our history shows clearly that admirable democratic ideas and motivations can lead to violence and unjustified killings. The striking thing about the Burns mob and the violent abolitionists was that they were driven by commendable democratic desires for liberty, rights, and direct civic participation. This is true of many uncivil disobedients.

[3] CBS News/*New York Times* Monthly Poll, April 1992, question 53.

[4] This uncivil streak has been called "bad" civil society. Chambers and Kopstein, "Bad Civil Society."

Angered by a disjunction between law and justice, uncivil disobedients are convinced the law can be redeemed by direct civic activism outside of established legal channels. Many violent uncivil disobedients are also committed to civic empowerment, believing that citizens in a democracy can and should change laws they believe are unjust. For the militant abolitionists in Boston, for instance, the Burns case brought the evil of the Fugitive Slave Act into focus and made its unjust consequences tangible and undeniable. The Boston abolitionists understood that they were morally implicated in the injustice of the Fugitive Slave Act: *their* police were being used to carry out its dictates, *their* courthouse jailed Burns, and *their* tax money was being spent to send a free man back to a life of chains.

Like the Boston mob, uncivil disobedients generally assume that, as citizens, they can exercise political authority and are responsible for making certain laws or legal actions accord with justice, as they see it. This can-do approach to politics is evident in the will to act. Consider, for instance, the fact that the Boston mob chose to act collectively to right a wrong. This may seem like a small thing in retrospect, but it is not. The decision to act—and, more specifically, to act together in the public realm without shame or remorse—suggests that the mob was an empowered group confident in its moral and political judgment. While members of the Boston mob certainly felt disempowered by the political situation and were acutely aware of the law's oppression and injustice, they did not accept this state of powerlessness. The Boston mob was neither composed of browbeaten subjects who had grown used to injustices nor of self-interested individuals who had ceased to care about public life. Rather, the mob was composed of *citizens* who felt a moral responsibility to make the law just and cared passionately about what legal officials were doing in their name. The mob assumed that it had a role to play in relation to the law. In this respect, the Boston mob was not obviously different from *civil* disobedients. Like civil disobedients, the Boston mob believed that citizens should be morally and politically involved in the laws that governed them. And, like civil disobedients, the abolitionist mob was stymied by institutional channels of change and, thus, acted outside of them.

Because uncivil disobedients complain bitterly about inefficiency, inadequacy, and corruption in political and legal institutions, it is logical to wonder if these charges have merit. This is an important question, first, because we may have more sympathy for uncivil disobedients if political institutions are failing them. Second, if political institutions are at the heart of the problem, then a means to address uncivil disobedience presents itself—that is, the reformation of political institutions, making them more efficient, responsive, competent, and honest. In some cases, most notably on the western frontier, political institutions were in shambles and vigilante complaints about inebriated judges, corrupted justices of the peace, and outlaw sheriffs had merit. In other cases like lynching in the post-Reconstruction South, the lynch mob's perception that the legal system was too lenient in applying the death penalty to African American defendants has not been borne out by statistical analysis.[5] In one major set of cases, then, institutional efficacy was low, while in another it was not.

The relationship between institutional efficacy and uncivil disobedience becomes more complicated still when we take cases like the Burns affair into account. As militant abolitionists in Boston saw it, the problem was not that political institutions were ineffective but rather that they were *too* effective. This was especially the case in Boston since the federal government was determined to make an example of Burns. President Franklin Pierce's orders were clear: "Incur any expense deemed necessary . . . to ensure the execution of the law."[6] In response, Secretary of War Jefferson Davis sent marines, cavalry, and artillery to make certain that Burns's procession from his jail cell to the Boston harbor was without incident. The show of force succeeded. Though an estimated fifty thousand individuals watched as Burns and a mass of federal guards processed through the streets of Boston, order was maintained and the law was enforced.

The Burns case and others like it suggest that the motivations behind uncivil disobedience are broader than the efficacy of political institutions. Uncivil disobedients are concerned about perceived injustices of the law and the legitimacy of legal and political institutions. What constitutes an injustice changes from case to case. Beliefs about whether the legal wrong was caused by political institutions that were too careless in executing their duties or too zealous in fulfilling them, too bloated with bureaucratic procedures or too inattentive to the requirements of due process, too willing to bend to contingencies or too formalistic and rigid also change from case to case. What does not change, however, is that the government is the object of enmity. Also unchanging across the cases is the steadfast belief that the corrective to institutional problems lies in shifting power away from legal institutions and officials and depositing it in the people.

The passionate call for liberty and the participatory democratic ideas elucidated by the Boston mob may have been commendable, but its results—violence and killing—were not. Looked at in terms of results and consequences, the picture of uncivil disobedients changes radically. They seem markedly different from civil disobedients. Rather than protests, sit-ins, and marches, the Boston mob took up a battering ram and used deadly force. And, rather than thinking carefully about tactics, the mob focused primarily on accomplishing its goal of freeing Burns. As Parker predicted in his speech at Faneuil Hall, ends trumped means.

[5] Tolnay and Beck, *Festival of Violence*, 86–118.
[6] Von Frank, *Trials of Anthony Burns*, 174.

The tendency of uncivil disobedients to engage in indiscriminate killings is of even greater concern. Not all uncivil disobedients have been arbitrary and unsystematic in the targets of their violence. Many frontier vigilantes only targeted individuals they believed to be guilty of wrongdoing. Though frontier vigilantes were swayed by racism and xenophobia and they certainly made errors in assessing guilt, many also made efforts to punish the appropriate individual. In the Burns affair, Frederick Douglass defended the killing of the guard along similar lines. The guard chose to be allied with a pro-slavery government, and he was actively assisting to send a free man back into slavery. As Douglass saw it, the guard was guilty. In this sense, violent uncivil disobedience is somewhat different from terrorism. The paradigmatic example of terrorism is a bomb on a bus: the explosion kills whoever happens to be on the bus, despite the fact that the woman riding the bus to work or the man running errands is not responsible for the political problem that the terrorists seek to remedy.[7] The violence is random and unassociated with guilt.

In other instances of uncivil disobedience, however, guilt has been a ruse and violence has been random. Some lynch mobs in the post-Reconstruction South killed innocent relatives when they could not locate the ostensibly guilty party. They strung up cousins, uncles, and brothers instead. Other southern lynching crowds made it clear that their goal was to terrorize local freedmen and -women into submission. In these cases and others, guilt is gutted of meaning. What, for instance, were the children killed in the bombing of the federal building in Oklahoma City guilty of? Absent guilt, the distinction between uncivil disobedience and terrorism is less apparent. To capture these points of similarity and dissimilarity and to acknowledge this movement from targeted violence to indiscriminate violence, I've called uncivil disobedience a homegrown version of terrorism. Regardless of what one calls it, it is important to note that the phenomenon has affinities with terrorism, though it is not exactly the same as terrorism.

A crucial question, then, is how have advantageous democratic motivations and ideas been twisted to justify indiscriminate violence? How has an impulse to make the law just and a desire for popular sovereignty facilitated random killing? The appearance of indiscriminate violence is crucial. It signals that democratic motivations and ideas have gone terribly awry. Moreover, it reveals a decisive difference between uncivil disobedience and its civil counterpart. Yet, the violence itself discloses very little about *how* democratic ideas have been distorted to justify the recourse to brute force. Arbitrary violence suggests that democratic ideas have been twisted to support malevolent ends, but it does not reveal what

[7] Walzer, *Just and Unjust Wars*, 197–206.

this twisting looks like. The observation that uncivil disobedients tend to see violence as legitimate while civil disobedients do not runs into a similar problem. In and of itself, this distinction reveals little about why some dissenting groups choose violence and others do not. Violence alone does not tell us very much about how uncivil disobedients have conceptualized law, citizenship, and popular sovereignty or how their conceptions of these key terms facilitated a turn toward random killing.

One way to address the role of democratic ideas in justifying indiscriminate violence is to look more closely at historical cases of uncivil disobedience. Many of the largest and most significant groups of domestic terrorists left copious documents defending their actions. These manifestos, constitutions, articles, diaries, editorials, books, poems, memoirs, and letters show us how uncivil disobedients understood the law, citizenship, and the relationship between citizens and legal officials. A "lay political theory" is revealed in these documents, if you will. The defenses and apologies for violent uncivil disobedience show how legal and political ideas operate at the bottom of the political pyramid, and how, more specifically, ideas can be adopted, appropriated, and manipulated by ordinary citizens. The "lay political theory" that emerges around uncivil disobedience is more intriguing and complex than one might expect. Uncivil disobedients are typically unschooled in canonical political theory and do not have an academic approach to political ideas. Yet, despite their lack of intellectual discipline and tradition, many uncivil disobedients are familiar with their nation's dominant political ideas and frameworks and feel free to use them in unexpected ways. Their political theory is startling, but it's not incoherent or inconsequential.

These cases of violent uncivil disobedience are instructive because they suggest that an activist approach to the law is not dangerous in and of itself. Rather, a *particular* conception of the relationship between citizens, laws, and legal institutions has opened the way to indiscriminate violence. Problems may arise when citizens think that the law ought to replicate popular will or morality as closely as possible. Parker, in his passionate speech to the abolitionists, hinted at this tight connection between law and morality or will when he urged the audience to enforce "the law of the people," that is, their immediate, personal understanding of justice in Burns's case rather than the government's distant and compromise-driven law. Other vigilantes and lynch mobs have carried Parker's logic further, arguing that vigilante "law" is purer than institutional law because it represents the will of the people or their morality in an unadulterated form. Uncivil disobedients tend to idealize the law as a mirror: The law should reflect their will or their morality without distortions or flaws. In their view then, the rule of the people should dominate the rule of law, and democracy should trump constitutionalism. This instrumental view of law as a mirror of popular sovereignty provokes a crisis mentality in which any discord between the law and popular will or morality becomes a catastrophe. Moreover, it prompts collective solipsism. While it would be too strong to say that uncivil disobedients truly think that they are the only things existent, they tend to act as if this were the case. They are apt to care only about their own will or morality in relation to the law, not that of others.

To put this point differently, problems may arise when citizens conceive of democracy as a series of perfect identity relationships. As uncivil disobedients see it, the governed should be identified with the government, the people should be identified with the law, and the law should be identified with justice. It's important to note that this emphasis on identification is not unique to uncivil disobedients. Carl Schmitt argued that "all democratic arguments rest logically on a series of identities . . . the identity of the governed and governing . . . the identity of the people with their representatives in parliament . . . the identity of the state and the law, and finally an identity of the quantitative (the numerical majority or unanimity) with the qualitative (the justice of the laws)." When these identities seem to hold, Schmitt suggested, the government seems democratic. Hence, policies and procedures that tighten the sense of identification between the governed with the governing, the people with law, and the law with justice—like, for instance, "extension of the suffrage, the reduction of electoral terms of office, the introduction of referenda and initiatives"—are elements of democratic governments.[8]

Schmitt noted that these democratic procedures and policies "can never reach an absolute, direct identity that is actually present at every moment." Absolute and perfect identification, he suggested, is a dream. Mundane democratic politics will never quite get to a point of precise identification in which, for example, the people can identify fully with law and see their will in it.[9] Cases of uncivil disobedience suggest that the problem is only partly the gap between the real (mundane politics) and the ideal (perfect identification). The deeper difficulty is with the ideal itself—that is, with the conception of democracy as a series of identifications. Cases of uncivil disobedience suggest that once this ideal is in play, it may be difficult to resist the logic of perfect identification and absolute equivalence. The gap between the real and the ideal can become intolerable, and the need to close it can be irresistible.

To explicate this problematic view of an activist approach to law and democracy, I examine three particularly prolific and well-documented groups whose disobedience degenerated into indiscriminate killings: vigilance committees on the American frontier, lynch mobs in the post-

[8] Schmitt, *Crisis of Parliamentary Democracy*, all quotations from 26–28.

[9] Indeed, Schmitt goes on to note "Democracy seems fated then to destroy itself in the problem of the formation of a will."

Reconstruction South, and militant abolitionists. In the first chapter's discussion of justifications for violence, I examine the contemporary militia movement. The order of my case studies breaks with chronology. Although the abolitionists preceded Western frontier vigilantes and lynch mobs historically, they follow these groups in my analysis. A portion of the abolitionist movement, radical political abolitionism, offers insight into early attempts at breaking the connection between legal activism and terrorism and a glimpse of a different conception of the relationship between democracy and constitutionalism that resists the dream of perfect identification with law. I draw out the implications of this embryonic idea of law in the conclusion.

Going Negative

It is important to say a few words about why examining this negative example of uncivil disobedience is a worthy enterprise. Why look at when things go wrong with democratic ideas and action, as opposed to when they go right? Why examine uncivil disobedients, groups of citizens who commit illegal and violent acts while claiming to uphold democratic ideals and serve justice? Most of the literature exploring disobedience as a political phenomenon and discussing the limits of an obligation to obey the law has focused instead on the more uplifting case of civil disobedience and, in particular, on the civil rights movement in the 1950s and 1960s. My approach is different. To the extent that I discuss civil disobedience, it is to illuminate the characteristics of uncivil disobedience. So, it makes a good deal of sense to ask why *this* focus.

First, instances of uncivil disobedience argue against moralizing democracy, claiming it as the ultimate positive political stance and flattening it into an unassailable force of good. Democracy is far more intriguing and complex by a good measure. Cases of uncivil disobedience underscore that complexity by showing that sound democratic ideas and motivations may not necessarily result in just outcomes. To chart the path between admirable democratic ideas and terrorism is, in some sense, to indict these ideas as being potentially dangerous. The notion that democratic ideas can be risky may seem strange in an era of exporting democracy to other parts of the globe. Yet, the Western canon of political thought is well populated with critics of democracy. They stress the instability of democracy's diffused schema of political power and its inclination toward internecine violence.

Tocqueville's "tyranny of the majority" tapped into (and tweaked) this tradition by suggesting that democratic aspirations toward uncontained popular sovereignty could be destructive. As Tocqueville saw it, an unimpeded popular sovereign could trample the rights of minorities and encourage a soul-crushing culture of conformity and homogeneity. The image of unconstrained popular sovereignty that Tocqueville left us with is that of an ouroboros, a snake eating its own tail. Like the ouroboros, Tocqueville's tyranny of the majority suggests that the very ideas that sustain democracy can lead to its destruction. In the spirit of Tocqueville's insight, democratic theorists should not shrink from exploring the unsavory outcomes of democratic ideas. Violent uncivil disobedience is one place to begin this work.

The push to spread democracy elsewhere—and the realization that exported versions will not be like the American version that we have today—underscores the need to explore the dangerous potential of democratic ideas. America's own history of uncivil disobedience will not, I think, provide too much specific insight into the troubling turn that democratic ideas could take in other regions of the world. Such results would be governed by culture, religion, and the political history of those individuals who pick up democratic ideas and, reinterpreting them anew, make these concepts their own. But, America's history of uncivil disobedience does urge humility, caution, and, most importantly, the recognition that democracy is a fragile and demanding form of government. Democracy requires a great deal from citizens. But its demands can be confusing and opaque. It can it be difficult for citizens to know precisely what is demanded of them or how to give it.

Second, cases of uncivil disobedience give a new vantage point on the fraught and complex relationship in liberal democracies between democracy and constitutionalism. Liberal democracies tend to ground their legitimacy in both the rule of law and the rule of people, and tend to claim that law and the will of the people are determinative. Yet, how can this be? What happens when law demands one course of action but people (or their representatives) demand another? Perhaps the people and their representative institutions should be passive before the requirements of law, understanding law as "an essential safeguard against the occasional ill humors in the society," as Alexander Hamilton put it in *The Federalist*, no. 78. This seeming solution shows the intractability of the problem, however. The idea that the rule of law should trump the rule of the people raises a question about the democratic character of the polity. If the rule of law always dominates the rule of the people, then in what sense are liberal democracies actually *democracies?* Moreover, it is harder to eliminate people from the rule of law than Hamilton's neat solution suggests. Arguing that the rule of law should trump leaves open a large question: Who should decide what the rule of law means? Law is not self-acting. It needs people for its construction, interpretation, and execution. This fact surreptitiously opens a back door to the rule of the people.

For the most part, two dominant approaches have been employed to explore the tension between democracy and constitutionalism. The first has been theoretical. Political and legal theorists have argued for particular normative conceptions of democracy and constitutionalism. They have also considered whether these values are truly at odds with one another. In general, the theoretical approach has tended toward abstraction and steered clear of historical cases or events. Jürgen Habermas, for instance, has emphasized the contradictory "idea that the addressees of the law must also be able to understand themselves as its authors" and that the will of the people must be bound to and constrained by reason.[10] Bonnie Honig has also analyzed the "tense relationship between constitutionalism and democracy" at the core of liberal democracies, "which take as their ground and goal both the rule of law and the rule of the people."[11] Others such as Stephen Holmes and Jeremy Waldron have considered the ways in which a "precommitment" view of constitutional constraints—that is, constraints rationally chosen by the people at some point in the past in anticipation of their irrational behavior in the future—facilitates or impinges on rule of the people.[12] Sheldon Wolin presents the tension between democracy and constitutionalism in starker terms and as two distinct kinds of politics: a "fugitive" eruption of democracy "conceived of as a moment of experience, a crystallized response to deeply felt grievances or needs on the part" of ordinary citizens and a governing form of representative politics that means "accommodating to bureaucratized institutions that, *ipso facto*, are hierarchical in structure and elitist, permanent rather than fugitive—in short, anti-democratic."[13] One side of this strained contradictory relationship implies identification between the people and law based on engagement and action, as the "authors" of the law express their "will" or "deeply felt grievances" in a "democracy." The other implies constraint and repose, as the "addressees" of the law are bound by the restrictions and "bureaucratized institutions" encompassed in "constitutionalism" and "the rule of law." Each presents risks. Constitutionalism can induce civic complacency and a dissipated sense of legitimacy. Fugitive democracy, as George Kateb observes, "may be only demotic," consisting of "a rage driven by resentment, envy, and rancor."[14]

The second approach to constitutionalism and democracy has been institutional. Political scientists and legal scholars have considered how

[10] Habermas, "Constitutional Democracy," 767.

[11] Honig, "Dead Rights, Live Futures," 792–93. Also see Honig, "Between Decision and Deliberation," 14.

[12] Holmes, *Passions and Constraint*, Waldron, "Precommitment and Disagreement." Also see Elster and Slagstad, *Constitutionalism and Democracy*.

[13] Wolin, *Politics and Vision*, 601–606. Also see Wolin, "Fugitive Democracy"; and Wolin, "Norm and Form."

[14] Kateb, "Wolin as a Critic of Democracy."

tension between constitutionalism and democracy has played out between the Supreme Court and the political branches. In contrast with the theoretical approach, this body of work is empirical and historical. Debates about judicial review have, for instance, focused on the "counter-majoritarian difficulty" or the Supreme Court's capacity to thwart "the will of representatives of the actual people of the here and now" and to exercise "control, not on behalf of the prevailing majority, but against it."[15] Addressing this tension, Bruce Ackerman has argued that the Constitution creates a dialectic system of politics: The mundane, day-to-day system of politics in which citizens are politically passive recipients of law is counterbalanced with transformative moments of higher law-making in which "We, the people" rule. Larry Kramer has more recently argued for a return to "popular constitutionalism," a practice in which the people have final interpretive authority over the Constitution, making courts and legislatures subordinate to their judgments.[16]

Cases of uncivil disobedience unsettle established ways of thinking about democracy and constitutionalism by examining them from an unexplored perspective, that of ordinary citizens. Like institutional scholarship on judicial review, these cases bring history to the fore, emphasizing how the tension between democracy and constitutionalism has been experienced in a particular historical context and how it has changed over time. Yet, the focus here is on citizens not institutions. To borrow Habermas's phrasing, the focus is on exploring how citizens can be both "authors" and "addressees" of the law. The virtue of this approach is that a tension that can seem abstract is made concrete and specific. Looking at cases of uncivil disobedience clarifies that radical popular sovereignty has been associated with making the law respond to justice, reasserting the rights of the people, and taking the law into one's own hands. Radical popular sovereignty has also been connected with open hostility to legal institutions and officers and with strong opposition to the idea that the sovereign people must be an "addressee" of the law. Likewise, it has been linked to the notion that the people should exert control over the law to make it reflect sovereign will (and in this sense "author" it). These cases remind us of a persistent appeal in the United States of uncoupling author from addressee. Through them, we can see a recurring dream of radical popular sovereignty as an escape from the rule of law and as pure, unmediated expression of popular will.

On a normative level, these cases also suggest caution about conceptually fragmenting the roles of author and addressee, as well as severing de-

[15] Bickel, *Least Dangerous Branch*, 17.
[16] Kramer, *People Themselves*.

mocracy from constitutionalism. They warn more specifically against imagining one role or one kind of rule as dominating and suppressing the other. This kind of thinking has been associated with a valorization of social and political homogeneity and with violence and antagonism toward those seen as different. As many vigilantes and lynch mobs saw it, the people had to be a cohesive and uniform group in order to legitimately express its will and to control the law. Thus, they celebrated their own uniformity and homogeneity, seeing themselves as united by similar civic and moral commitments and often linked by racial bonds. Likewise, many vigilantes and lynch mobs were hostile to dissent from within their own ranks and intolerant of anyone who might erode the perception that they acted as one sovereign people with one cohesive will. The connection between the idea (elevating the rule of the people over the rule of law) and the action (intolerance of dissent and difference) is not causal. Still, it has been repeated enough times to give one pause.

Third, examining cases of uncivil disobedience exposes and clarifies the gray area that exists between lawful and lawless actions. Uncivil disobedients have repeatedly situated themselves in this gray area by claiming to break the law in a lawlike manner. As one apologist of frontier vigilantism put it, "vigilance becomes omnipotent, not as a usurper, but as a friend in an emergency . . . and if law must be broken to save the state, then it breaks it soberly, conscientiously, and under the formulas of law."[17] Some uncivil disobedients have gone further by denying "that the word 'crime' should be applied to lynchings at all. Such a crime, condoned by the people, cannot be a crime, since people make the law."[18] Though it is clear that uncivil disobedients do violate law, it is harder to reject that their ideas and rationalizations are often bound up with law in intriguing ways. Frontier vigilantes conducted elaborate trials, for instance, in which judges were elected, witnesses called to the stand, and prosecutorial attorneys made closing arguments to the jury. Militant abolitionists arguments were also deeply enmeshed in the legal categories, critiques of the Constitution, and analysis of legal precedent.

The historical and legal scholarship on vigilantism and lynching has also emphasized that these groups seem to be inside and outside of the law. Influenced by the scholarship of Eric Hobsbawm, George Rudé, and Charles Tilly, who have stressed the importance of studying collective violence and the rational and purposeful nature of crowds, contemporary scholars have noted that vigilantes and lynch mobs typically garnered the approval of the community. Indeed, Robert Maxwell Brown has demonstrated that vigilantes even garnered the approval of the legal community,

[17] Bancroft, *Works of Hubert Howe Bancroft*, 36:10.
[18] Waldrep, *The Many Faces of Judge Lynch*, 187.

and, in this sense, their acts can be described as "lawless lawfulness."[19] Moreover, scholars have noted that vigilantes and lynch mobs were seen as legitimate because their actions were participatory and public. As Lawrence Friedman noted about frontier vigilantism, "the 'respectable' citizens—the majority perhaps—in western towns were not really lawless. Quite to the contrary, people were accustomed to law and order."[20] John Phillip Reid has found evidence that pioneers "outside" of the law on the overland trail were scrupulously attentive to property rights and contracts, and that they were careful to establish popular acceptance of informal punishments on the trail.[21] Vigilante political rhetoric, Linda Gordon has observed, "frequently takes us back to the source of authority, and more specifically to the vigilantes' conviction that the popular will transcends the law. They do not despise the law, but only supersede it, overrule it, when it has deviated from its duty to express the popular will."[22]

Yet how could uncivil disobedients truly be lawless and lawful? How could they be inside and outside law at the same time? This question clearly runs into the thorny issue of political legitimacy. To be answered fully, it requires a judgment of just how much political legitimacy a particular group of uncivil disobedients has. It may also demand thoroughgoing assessment of the legitimacy of extra-legislative action by the people—what Gordon Wood has referred to as "the people out-of-doors"[23]—in American politics. Such an assessment is likely to vary a great deal depending on the historical context, the alleged injustice that prompted the uncivil disobedience, and the consequences of it. No historical context, it seems to me, would make indiscriminate violence toward uninvolved individuals legitimate. Even uncivil disobedience that avoids this type of violence has been harmful to American democracy and dangerous to some of its central precepts. Certain acts of uncivil disobedience might be legitimate nonetheless. In this respect the Burns case gives us much to think about. Was the storming of the courthouse to rescue Burns legitimate? These are questions of great consequence. To address them sufficiently requires a different kind of analysis and approach than I undertake here.

A narrower approach to illuminating the shadowy position of uncivil disobedients in relation to law is to examine more closely how they violate law. Uncivil disobedience is a particular kind of dissent. It is not random, but rather follows a pattern of law breaking. As such, it is essential to determine what kind of laws uncivil disobedients typically violate. Criminal laws? Civil laws? Constitutional laws? Local laws? State laws?

[19] See chapter 6, "Lawless Lawfulness" in Brown, *Strain of Violence*.
[20] Friedman, *History of American Law*, 277.
[21] Reid, *Law for the Elephant; Policing the Elephant*.
[22] Gordon, *The Great Arizona Orphan Abduction*, 256–57.
[23] Wood, *Creation of the American Republic*, 319.

To ask this question somewhat differently, how are uncivil disobedients distinct from other kinds of lawbreakers? Uncivil disobedients are different from common criminals, who break law solely for personal gain. They are also distinct from pirates and bandits, who purposely operate beyond the boundary of law. Uncivil disobedients are not the same as revolutionaries, who break law with the hope of establishing an entirely new legal regime.

One crucial distinction of uncivil disobedients' lawlessness stands out: Uncivil disobedients tend to shelve second-order rules governing who is empowered to interpret, adjudicate, and enforce law. To use H.L.A. Hart's useful distinction, they disregard power-conferring rules.[24] By this, I mean that uncivil disobedients attempt to suspend the rules dictating that certain individuals and institutions are authorized to judge and enforce law (judges, lawyers, police officers, sheriffs, courts, and so on). As they see it, the sovereign people ultimately govern power-conferring rules and, thus, the people preside over legal officials as well. By the same logic, uncivil disobedients tend to be dismissive of the idea of accepting punishment for breaking the law. Why should the people be punished for asserting its sovereign will? Why should a self-governing people be penalized for doing what it thinks is right? Focusing on power-conferring rules provides a sharper picture of the gray area of "lawful lawlessness" that is characteristic of acts of dissent and resistance. If we imagine a continuum that stretches from obedience of the law to outright revolution, uncivil disobedience lies in between civil disobedience and revolution. Uncivil disobedients are more lawless than civil disobedients, who typically do not intercede in power-conferring rules, and less lawless than revolutionaries, who hope to radically alter existing power-conferring rules not just suspend them. Particular historic groups of uncivil disobedients are arguably more like civil disobedients, while others are more like revolutionaries. Still, uncivil disobedience is a type of dissent that is distinct from civil disobedience and revolution in important respects.

Focusing on power-conferring rules also clarifies a common difference drawn between uncivil and civil disobedients: the acceptance of punishment. A number of political theorists have argued that civil disobedience is legitimate in part if it involves accepting the given punishment for one's crimes. The history of uncivil disobedience suggests this basis of legitimacy is problematic. Consider, for instance, the case of a post-reconstruction lynch mob that killed a brother or uncle or whomever it could find in the place of the alleged offender. It is difficult to imagine that accepting the punishment would make the killing legitimate. Emphasizing that civil disobedients should perform certain actions like willingly accepting punish-

[24] Hart, *Concept of Law*.

ment can potentially obscure why these actions matter. There is a risk of fixating on the act at the expense of the thinking behind it. Accepting punishment is significant because it reveals an approach to law in general (and power-conferring rules in particular) that is markedly different from that of uncivil disobedients. Civil disobedients accept the law as an external limitation. Unlike uncivil disobedients, they tend to understand democracy and constitutionalism as entwined, and to conceptualize autonomy as bound up with domination. Uncivil disobedients pull the rule of the people and the law apart. Civil disobedients hold these values in tension, breaking the law as an act of democratic autonomy and submitting to it as well. Focusing less on the act and more on what it reveals also suggests that there may be other acts of dissent that hold democracy and constitutionalism in tension. Accepting the punishment is one way to do this. It may not be the only way.

When the Boston mob picked up its battering ram and together forced it through the courthouse door, it joined a larger group of uncivil disobedients who have violently opposed laws they believed to be unjust. In a sense, the chapters follow this battering ram as it moves from group to group throughout American history. The reason these groups have battered down law's door have varied considerably. The Boston mob assaulted its courthouse door to save an African American man; others in the post-Reconstruction South broke down courthouse doors to kill African American men and women. These are vital distinctions. But they should not overshadow the broad similarity of the tactics and approaches to the law among uncivil disobedients. They should not stop us from considering why this form of dissent has at times turned into a kind of terrorism. Nor should they deter us from exploring the role of democratic ideas in a turn to terrorism. And, to address the questions, we need to look less at the battering ram and more at the groups that have wielded it.

Chapter One

VIOLENCE, AMERICAN STYLE

ASKED TO DESCRIBE THE MILITIA MOVEMENT, one member put it this way: "We're like libertarians on steroids, but we're not nuts. We are totally against overthrowing the federal government."[1] The first sentence of this statement seems clear. More so than the average American, militia members are adherents of individual liberty, personal responsibility, and a free market economy. They see these values as both imperative and in need of protection. This asssessment was echoed by an even more colorful compatriot, who noted that the militia movement is composed of "people sitting there with 'don't tread on me' stamped across their foreheads."[2]

What, though, does the second sentence in the first quotation mean? On the available evidence, it is possible to think that this militia member is either being a bit deceptive or a bit humorous (or perhaps some of each). If the movement is "totally against overthrowing the federal government," then why do its members regularly crawl around on their bellies with weapons at the ready in mock skirmishes? Why do members stockpile guns and antagonize government officials? Why, in short, do they spend hours and hours preparing for battle with their forsworn enemy, the government, if they are not itching for a fight?

There is, I think, good reason to believe that this militia member was not being disingenuous in his characterization of the movement as skittish of revolution. His sentiment is echoed throughout the movement. Members counterintuitively describe the militia movement as gun-happy and revolution-shy. It is difficult to see the advantage of deception on this point for the movement. If it hoped to lull the government into complacency in order to launch a surprise revolutionary attack, then its duplicity failed. The federal government has taken the threat presented by the militia movement quite seriously. Moreover, the movement has not been particularly secretive or stealthy. Rather than slinking around in the shadows in order to foment revolution, it has sought attention. Militia-movement members openly proclaim their positions on numerous garish Internet websites, they conduct interviews with the press, and they publish pamphlets, books, and manifestos. They have sought attention in other ways

[1] Hamilton, *Militias in America*, 49.

[2] Abanes, *American Militias*, 19.

too. One of the first actions of the Michigan Militia was to march onto a playground in Pellston, Michigan, wearing battle fatigues and carrying weapons. Part of a campaign called Operation Visibility, the Michigan Militia clearly hoped it would be seen.

Accepting the militia member's characterization of the movement as genuine raises a knotty question. What *is* the militia movement after? What does it hope to gain? If its goal is not to incite revolution, then what is its goal? This question applies to uncivil disobedients more generally because these groups have also typically disavowed a revolutionary agenda and stopped short of revolutionary action. The standard political equation of angry men + guns + collective action = revolution does not accurately describe vigilantes, lynch mobs, violent opponents of abortion, or radical environmentalists either.

One way to address this question is to examine what the militia movement says it wants and how it justifies its violence. Explanations of why violence is necessary often hold clues to its purpose. In explaining the recourse to brute force, militia members reveal what is at stake in it. The movement's violent goals can be sharpened further by placing them alongside two well-known justifications for revolutionary violence, Jean-Paul Sartre's defense of colonial violence in his preface to *The Wretched of the Earth* and John Locke's defense of revolutionary violence at the close of *Two Treatises of Government*. Sartre and Locke provide two sharply contrasting accounts of what revolutionary violence is for and how it should be justified. This contrast serves militia-movement justifications well, revealing more clearly what the movement hopes to gain through its violent collective action.

The Pull of the Past: Retrospective Justifications for Violence

There have been many violent uncivil disobedients throughout American history, and, as one might expect, each group has crafted its own defense of the necessity of violence based on the particular context.[3] Each group's justification for violence is rooted in a specific time and place and, of course, in the distinct political goals of the group. The justifications offered by lynch mobs in the post-Reconstruction South, for instance, differ sharply in their content from those offered by contemporary violent pro-life groups.

[3] The frequent occurrence of individual and collective violence throughout American history has raised questions about whether America is especially prone to bloodshed. See, for instance, Graham and Gurr, eds., *Violence in America*. Others have questioned whether democracy as a regime is prone to violence. See Rapoport and Weinberg, eds., *The Democratic Experience and Political Violence*.

The structure of these rationales is less varied, however. In particular, uncivil disobedients tend to justify their violence in conventional terms. These conventional justifications are striking and, as many commentators have noted, puzzling.[4] What's odd is that uncivil disobedients couple the extreme tactic of violence with traditional political concepts like law, rights, liberty, freedom, and popular sovereignty. What's more, uncivil disobedients have claimed that they are paragons of good citizenship and steadfast supporters of the American political tradition. Looked at in terms of what they do, uncivil disobedients are radical. Looked at in terms of what they say, uncivil disobedients are unexpectedly traditional. It has been difficult to figure out, therefore, if uncivil disobedients are defenders of traditional political institutions or rebels who hope to undermine the established political order.[5] The resulting picture of uncivil disobedients is akin to a child's flip book in which the head of an elephant or seal can be joined to the body of a lion or giraffe. In this case, the tongues of patriots are incongruously grafted onto the bodies of rebels.[6]

The contemporary militia movement, a loose collection of paramilitary groups on the far right of American politics, provides a particularly apt example of the conventional rhetoric of uncivil disobedients.[7] Formed in the mid-1990s, the militia movement describes itself as a defender of traditional freedoms and values against an increasingly oppressive government. Militia members argue that the U.S. government has turned against its foundational democratic values by adopting a series of repressive measures, including gun-control legislation, income-tax policy, and environmentally driven restrictions on private property. Because it is a grassroots organization without a central governing authority, the movement encompasses a range of views and approaches. Some segments of the militia

[4] See, for instance, Brown, *Strain of Violence*; Ingalls, *Urban Vigilantes in the New South*, 2–20; Rosenbaum and Sederberg, *Vigilante Politics*, 3–29.

[5] In an effort to capture this contradiction between what uncivil disobedients say and what they do, for instance, Rosenbaum and Sederberg refer to vigilantism as "establishment violence." Rosenbaum and Sederberg, *Vigilante Politics*.

[6] This incongruity may not be unique to uncivil disobedients. As Benjamin Barber notes, "Americans often appear to be both cynical and idealistic. How many American archetypes are at once both base and noble? The Pioneer . . . the Vigilante, even the Founder: each is a compromised idealist, a cynical naïf, a noble aggressor, a creative appropriator, an anomaly of nature with a beast's body and a divine head." Barber, *Strong Democracy*, 81.

[7] As with many extremist groups, the militia movement's size has been difficult to ascertain. Chip Berlet and Mathew Lyons estimate that at its height in the mid-1990s the antigovernment movement included 5 million individuals, with militia movement membership at about twenty to sixty thousand. Berlet and Lyons, *Right-Wing Populism in America*, 288. Richard Abanes estimates militia membership as high as 5 to 12 million while Neil A. Hamilton estimates that the movement was no larger than one hundred thousand. Abanes, *American Militias*, 2; Hamilton, *Militias in America*, 29. Most commentators agree, however, that the militia movement has been sharply on the decline since 1998.

movement openly espouse racist and anti-Semitic views about a Jewish-dominated government and conspiratorial "New World Order."[8] Other segments of the movement adamantly refuse to single out a racial or ethnic group for blame and are pointedly inclusive in their membership policies. Some portions of the movement tend toward paranoia and relish in spinning elaborate conspiratorial theories. Other portions of the movement meticulously stick to established facts and seem genuinely concerned about what they see as an overbearing government. Despite the diversity of views and approaches, the movement is united in its belief that citizens, taking arms against their government, can effectively check government oppression. The most dramatic and deadly example of this sort of violent populist check (which was praised by some in the movement and disavowed by others) occurred on April 19, 1995, when Timothy McVeigh and Terry Nichols bombed a federal building in Oklahoma City and killed 168 individuals.

The militia movement's particular beliefs and political agendas are not shared by other uncivil disobedients. It is difficult to imagine finding substantive political agreement at the policy level between the movement and other uncivil disobedients like, for instance, radical eco-terrorists, the Black Panthers, or the militant abolitionists. If we move back from the details of the movement's positions, however, some general and representative tendencies emerge. In particular, the movement offers a conventional justification for violence that is characteristic of uncivil disobedience in three ways. Like other uncivil disobedients, the movement legitimates its violence by arguing that fundamental political pacts and promises have been broken, by appealing to the past, and by depicting its violence as reformist rather than revolutionary.

Promises, Promises

Underneath the convoluted conspiracy theories and elaborate interpretations of American law, the militia movement's anger has a simple source: broken promises. The broken promises vary, ranging from commitments to national sovereignty, protections of individual rights, and assurances of fair fiscal policy. The violator of these pacts is unchanging, however. It is the government. Consider the militia movement's persistent attacks on gun-control legislation. As the movement has framed it, a fundamen-

[8] According to the Southern Poverty Law Center, "Of the 441 militia and 368 Patriot groups that existed between 1994 and 1996, 137 had ties to the racist right." Dees and Corcoran, *Gathering Storm*, 200. Many of the precursors for the contemporary militia movement, such as the John Birch Society, the Liberty Lobby, and the Posse Comitatus, have been labeled racist and anti-Semitic as well. On the influence of Christianity on the movement, see Juergensmeyer, *Terror in the Mind of God*, 19–43.

tal problem with restrictions on firearms ownership is that it violates a promise made by the government in the Second Amendment of the Constitution.[9] According to the movement, the Second Amendment should be interpreted according to the original intent of the founders.[10] As the movement sees it, the Second Amendment enshrines the natural right of American citizens to possess guns and, if need be, to organize themselves into armed groups (militias) in order to protect themselves from government oppression. In addition, the movement argues that the amendment also limits the government from regulating, monitoring, or generally interfering with citizens purchasing, owning, or using firearms.[11] And, adhering to a well-established tenet of natural rights theory, movement members argue that the government's violation of this natural right limits their duty to obey. If the government fails to uphold its promise, they argue, what duty do they have to obey its laws?

By their own account then, the movement's dispute with the American government concerns a vow and its violation. The movement, in remembering and honoring the constitutional promise enshrined in the Second Amendment, argues that it is more loyal to the Constitution and the nation's foundational values than the government is.[12] Militia-movement members are especially attached to the Constitution, which, in their view, confirms the government's deceit and validates the rectitude of their position. It is not unusual to find elaborate analyses of the Second Amendment and its relation to the rest of the Constitution in militia-movement manifestos, documents, and essays. What's more, some militia members carry a diminutive version of the Constitution in their shirt pockets as a sign of their fidelity to it.[13]

The first thing to note about the militia movement's interpretation of the Second Amendment is that it is not as odd or extremist as one might

[9] The Second Amendment reads, "A well regulated militia being necessary to the security of a free State, the right of the People to keep and bear arms shall not be infringed."

[10] It is important to note that originalism is a well-established form of interpretation outside of the militia movement. Bork, "Neutral Principles and Some First Amendment Problems"; Meese, "Interpreting the Constitution"; Rakove, *Original Meanings*; Whittington, *Constitutional Interpretation.*

[11] The Supreme Court, in contrast, has interpreted the Second Amendment as establishing the right of states to organize armed militias like the National Guard. The Court reads the amendment as establishing a collective right not an individual one, and it understands that the amendment empowers government rather than limiting it. For the Supreme Court's interpretation of the Second Amendment, see *Miller v. Texas, 153 U.S. 535 (1894)*; *Presser v. Illinois, 116 U.S. 252 (1886)*; *U.S. v. Cruikshank, 92 U.S. 542 (1876)*; *U.S. v. Miller, 307 U.S. 174 (1939).*

[12] Michael Barkun's description of the movement's anti-statism and its sense of patriotic superiority is particularly evocative and persuasive. Barkun, "Violence in the Name of Democracy."

[13] Dyer, *Harvest of Rage*, 146.

first think. A number of prominent liberal constitutional law scholars such as Sanford Levinson, Akil Reed Amar, and Laurence Tribe have argued that the Second Amendment should be interpreted as protecting an individual right. Though these scholars do not adopt an originalist interpretation of the Second Amendment and do not believe the right to keep and bear arms is an absolute right, they have come to the same general conclusion about its meaning. What's more, this understanding of the Second Amendment may be gaining institutional traction. In March 2007, for the first time in U.S. history, a federal appeals court struck down a gun-control law on Second Amendment grounds in *Parker v. District of Columbia*.

The movement's originalist interpretation of the Second Amendment and its nostalgia for the founding period tends to work against its larger goal of resisting government oppression. As the movement sees it, the Second Amendment should spark memories of an American Revolution in which scrappy farmers, turned citizen-soldiers, resisted tyranny against all odds armed only with the farm firearm.[14] The movement thinks about contemporary gun-control legislation, then, by taking a nostalgic turn and attempting to understand the Second Amendment as the founders did in the eighteenth century. Yet this originalist reading strategy undercuts the movement's strategic capacity to check the government. Is today's farmer armed with a gun an effective deterrent to government oppression? It seems clear that armed individuals bent on protecting their rights can become a nuisance to the government; they may even be able to create a climate of instability, fear, and chaos. It's less clear, however, that a farmer armed with a gun—or, even a collection of farmers with a cache of guns—can effectively deter government oppression. The conflicts at Ruby Ridge, Idaho and Waco, Texas, both of which are discussed widely within the movement, seem to make this point explicitly.[15] If effectively resisting an oppressive government were the goal, it would make more sense to read the Second Amendment in contemporary terms, and the Constitution as a so-called living document. Why fight a twenty-first-century government armed with bombs, tanks, aircraft, battleships, and nuclear weapons as well as thousands of personnel trained in their use with an eighteenth-century strategy of a farmer and his gun?

My point is not to snipe at the movement from the sidelines or chastise it for inconsistency, but rather, to show that the movement is deeply attached to the idea of the Second Amendment as a sacred promise from the past, so much so that other equally logical approaches are out of the ques-

[14] It is important to note that this idea of scrappy farmers, turned citizen-soldiers, is deeply masculine. Snyder, *Citizen-Soldiers and Manly Warriors*.

[15] For another example of the inadequacy of firearms, see Wendy Brown's discussion of the bombing of MOVE in Philadelphia. Brown, "Guns, Cowboys, Philadelphia Mayors and Civic Republicanism."

tion. Indeed, the conception of the Second Amendment as an inviolable promise from the past is central to the movement's understanding of the political world. Moreover, the movement's mission of holding the government accountable for violating this vow is crucial to its own sense of legitimacy.

Given the movement's goal to gain political sympathy from other citizens, however, its fixation on a broken promise is prudent. As justifications for violence go, a broken promise certainly has some bite in American politics. The American revolutionaries were successful at making this sort of argument, claiming that their radical measures were justified because England violated the rights promised to them as Englishmen. Other uncivil disobedients have also relied on the idea of a broken vow. Vigilantes on the frontier, for instance, argued that the government had reneged on its fundamental promise to protect its citizens and justified their violence in terms of the natural right to self-preservation.[16] Many abolitionists also framed their case in terms of natural rights and political perfidy. Radical political abolitionists like Lysander Spooner, for instance, contended that the Constitution supported emancipation and that current government officials were morally and constitutionally compelled to deliver on this promise.[17] Still others like Frederick Douglass focused on the Declaration of Independence, arguing that slavery violated the fundamental rights and promises established in this foundational document. The way to rectify this wrong, according to Douglass, was to honor the initial agreement.[18]

Past Perfect

The tendency of uncivil disobedients to think in terms of broken vows is related to another general characteristic—that is, to think in terms of the past. If the outlook of uncivil disobedients can be ascribed a direction, it is decidedly backward looking. They are nostalgic scavengers who dust

[16] Bancroft, *Works*, see vols. 36 and 37; Brown, *Strain of Violence*; Dimsdale, *The Vigilantes of Montana*.

[17] Spooner, *The Collected Works of Lysander Spooner*. Though their position on the Constitution was antithetical to the radical political abolitionists, the Garrisonian abolitionists also understood the Constitution as a political promise that bound the people and their government. See, for instance, Phillips, *Review of Lysander Spooner's Essay on the Unconstitutionality of Slavery*; and *Constitution a Pro-Slavery Compact*.

[18] See, for instance, Douglass's jeremiad "What to the Slave Is the Fourth of July?" Like Douglass, many other political radicals on the left have focused on the Declaration. See Lynd, *Intellectual Origins of American Radicalism*. For another abolitionist argument about the importance of the Declaration, see Phillips, *Constitution a Pro-Slavery Compact*, 93–94. For earlier abolitionist references to the Declaration, see Foner, *We, the Other People*, 13–14.

off ideals and values that they believe have been forgotten. While uncivil disobedients may reinterpret these old ideals and values and use them in unexpected ways, their political vision generally is not creative or novel. Past principles are often significantly tweaked by the group's radicalism, and American history is frequently interpreted in an unfamiliar (and, at times, questionable) manner. These principles and this history may seem unrecognizable. But, these are reworkings of the past. Rather than advancing an original political project, uncivil disobedients revise, reconsider, and reconstruct.

For the militia movement this retrospective outlook manifests itself foremost in its tendency to package its contemporary grievances as recurrent problems throughout American history. Consider Timothy McVeigh's letter published in 1992 in the *Union-Sun and Journal* in Lockport, New York, that frames McVeigh's current complaints in terms of the past. "We have no proverbial tea to dump," McVeigh observed. "Is a Civil War imminent? Do we have to shed blood to reform the current system? I hope it doesn't come to that! But it might."[19] McVeigh might be faulted for his muddy historical comparisons. Are the militias more like the American revolutionaries or the combatants of the Civil War? And, if it is the latter, what side of this war does the movement resemble, the North, home of McVeigh's hero John Brown, or the South? The meaning of McVeigh's historical comparison is not entirely clear. What is clear, however, is that McVeigh understands the problems the militia movement intends to solve as having recurred throughout American history. Like McVeigh, members of the movement are much more likely to seek inspiration from Thomas Jefferson, James Madison, George Mason, John Adams, and Samuel Adams than contemporary political thinkers, that is, the Sartres of their day. Indeed, they have no Sartre and no need for one either.

In the militia movement's view, the conflict they face is an old one, as is its solution. There is nothing new under the sun. As one leader put it, "The usurpation of power on the part of the regime—not a government—but the regime that is in place is about to unfold into a very evil flower." In particular, it "is the ambition of our enemy . . . to destroy the Constitution and the Bill of Rights." Quoting Patrick Henry, the speaker added, "If we wish to be free, we must fight. We must fight. An appeal to arms and God is all that is left to us. All that is left to us."[20] As another militia member put it, "When a tyrant's brutality is not reigned in by justice, you will have somebody out there . . . to balance the scales of justice."[21]

[19] McVeigh's letter, published in 1992, is quoted in Dyer, *Harvest of Rage*, 221–22. On the retrospective quality of the militia movement, also see Garry Wills's argument that it represents an extreme articulation of a "Lockean orthodoxy in our political thinking," Wills, *A Necessary Evil*, 15 and 19.

[20] Abanes, *American Militias*, 2.

[21] Hamilton, *Militias in America*, 103.

The movement's retrospective approach is not unique. Lincoln described a similar tendency among the uncivil disobedients of his day, antebellum mobs in the North and South that attacked local ne'er-do-wells and reprobates in the 1830's. In Lincoln's view, this violence attempted to mimic the passion and shared sense of purpose that the founding generation experienced in the Revolution. Lincoln unequivocally disapproved of this fascination with America's revolutionary past: "[T]he scenes of the revolution . . . must fade upon the memory of the world, and grow more and more dim by the lapse of time."[22] Segments of the labor movement in the nineteenth century disagreed, arguing that the American Revolution was an apt example for the workingman. As Seth Luther, who was known as the Tom Paine of the labor movement, put it: "The workingmen bared their arms and bosoms in '76 and they are about to do it again in '36. . . . We will try the ballot box first. If that will not effect our righteous purpose, the next and last resort is the cartridge box."[23]

Over a century later, Malcolm X tapped into a similar revolutionary impulse in his speech "The Black Revolution." In contrast to Lincoln's criticism of the desire to return to the Revolution, Malcolm X embraced it. In his view, the Revolutionaries' willingness to use violence revealed their deep commitment to liberty. He urged black nationalists to adopt an analogous approach: There "are 22 million African-Americans who are ready to fight for independence right here. . . . If George Washington didn't get independence for the country nonviolently, and if Patrick Henry didn't come up with a nonviolent statement, and you taught me to look upon them as patriots and heroes, then it's time for you to realize that I have studied your books well."[24] Malcolm X's statement is particularly intriguing because, excised of the reference to the plight of African Americans, it could easily be confused for a pronouncement by the militia movement.[25] Given how different the goals of these two groups are, this is a remarkable connection. Both groups embraced the Revolution and, contrary to Lincoln's advice, attempted to revive its passion, united sense of purpose, and the legitimacy of its violence.

Revolution Lite

A significant distinction needs to be made, however, between wanting to initiate a revolution and wanting to reexperience aspects of the American Revolution. Uncivil disobedients tend toward the latter. While uncivil

[22] Basler, *Collected Works of Abraham Lincoln*, 1: 114–15.

[23] Foner, *We, the Other People*, 9–10. On labor violence in the nineteenth century, see Louis Adamic's discussion on the early labor riots and the Molly Maguires in *Dynamite*, 3–20.

[24] Breitman, *Malcolm X Speaks*, 49. On the importance of the Revolution to early vigilante groups, see Brown, *Strain of Violence*, 41–66.

[25] See, for instance, Wood, *Panthers and the Militias*.

disobedients certainly admire the American Revolution, they typically shy away from the ambitious agenda of true revolutionaries. They might be accurately called "revolutionaries lite." They generally want to experience the action, excitement, zeal, shared sense of purpose, or self-determination encompassed in a revolution. At the same time, they shrink from the responsibility of constructing a new regime. Revolutions are, of course, serious undertakings. Successful revolutionaries must not only provide a persuasive critique of the current political structure but also provide a new and appealing vision of politics. They must convince others that they have a new political vision and that they are capable of actualizing that vision. Uncivil disobedients never go that far. They want the *feeling* of a revolution without the substance of one. Looked at in terms of their goals, uncivil disobedients are reformers who want to nudge the current political system backward rather than change it altogether. They use violence as the nudge, and their extreme methods might seem to imply an extreme agenda, but this is actually not the case. Compared to revolutionaries, their goals are modest, even reserved.[26]

The militia movement, for instance, has repeatedly emphasized its reformist goals and taken every opportunity to argue that it uses violence to coerce the government into changing specific policies. It espouses a carrot-and-stick approach to politics. There is no dream of a new carrot or a new stick. In a revealing explanation of the movement, one militia member observed that when "the people fear the government we will have tyranny." But, "when the government fears the people we will have liberty."[27] The goal is fear, not radical change. Even McVeigh in his editorial letter to the *Union-Sun and Journal* decried the need to *reform* the current system rather than change it entirely, asking "Do we have to shed blood to reform the current system?" The man responsible for the single most significant act of domestic terrorism within American borders prior to the September 11 attacks hoped to amend government for the better.

The same is true of other uncivil disobedients. Lynch mobs in the South and West pursued a specific goal, the killing of an offender. And, once they achieved this goal, the violence generally ceased. The abolitionists of the 1830s and 1840s occasionally flirted with the idea of extensive political change. But for the most part, they were wedded to a limited (albeit ambitious) agenda of ending the domestic slave trade, eliminating slavery in federally controlled areas, and convincing slave holders to support abolitionist legislation.

[26] As David Apter observes, "No matter how radical its objectives extra-institutional protest tends to be reformist rather than disjunctive in its consequences if not in its objectives." Apter, *Legitimization of Violence*, 10.

[27] Cozic, *Militia Movement*, 10.

The labor movement in the nineteenth century also pursued a pragmatic, reformist course even in its violent moments. Labor struggled, for instance, to establish an eight-hour workday, to end the use of convict labor in mines, to increase wages, and to establish job security. Even the Molly Maguires, a violent group of Irish miners in the anthracite-coal region of Pennsylvania that successfully terrorized mining supervisors in the late 1860s and early 1870s, had straightforward and down-to-earth demands. They used violence to halt supervisors from cheating on the measurement of coal and thus cheating on miners' wages, to force owners to address safety concerns, and to ensure that Irish miners were assigned to easy jobs in the mines.[28] Uncivil disobedients have had a range of goals, some reprehensible, others admirable. But regardless of what those goals were, they have been restricted and finite. From a truly revolutionary perspective, these goals might even be called paltry and piecemeal.[29]

Sartre's Prospective Justification for Violence

At first glance, Sartre's well-known defense of revolutionary violence in his preface to Frantz Fanon's *The Wretched of the Earth* would seem to offer insight into uncivil disobedience. Sartre's focus in this work is on violence that originates in the citizenry, not in the state, and no contemporary political theorist has written about violence from the political bottom with as much passion and approbation. It is somewhat surprising, then, that Sartre's justification for political violence falls flat in the American context. But in this case, the discord between the theory and practice is instructive. It reinforces the special backward character of uncivil disobedients' justifications for violence. It also suggests their violence is directed toward changing the location of legitimate power, not the notion of legitimate power.

In the preface, Sartre confronts a question like those posed by uncivil disobedients: How can political violence from below be justified? Sartre's answer to this question is unequivocal. Violence is warranted when it serves to generate new political identities and, as a result, when it produces a new political order. The justification for violence comes from its capacity to transform the "wretched of the earth" into free men who, by virtue of this cataclysmic change, can no longer be subjects of colonial

[28] Adamic, *Dynamite*, 9–20.

[29] As Nancy Rosenblum observes, there may be a virtue in what I have called "revolution lite." Associations like militias "may serve the purpose of containment. They can provide safety valves. Associations can circumscribe exhibitions of hate and hostile outbreaks of envy. Loathsome groups can be lifelines." Rosenblum, *Membership and Morals,* 22.

rule. In Sartre's terms, violence is the means through which the colonized "rediscovers his lost innocence and he comes to know himself in that he himself creates his self." When the peasant takes a gun in hand, "the old myths grow dim and the prohibitions are one by one forgotten." Using the weapon, the peasant for the first time "feels a *national* soil under his foot" and, in this moment of violence, "the Nation does not shrink from him; wherever he goes, wherever he may be, she is; she follows and is never lost to view, for she is at one with his liberty."[30]

What in part makes this bloodshed legitimate for Sartre is that it is not merely a method of reform. Legitimate violence is not politics by other means. Rather, the rebel's violence is justified if he understands it as a mechanism of radically and irrevocably altering himself and his country. He must realize that killing is politically transformative and therapeutic. As Sartre infamously put it, the rebel must believe that "to shoot down a European is to kill two birds with one stone, to destroy an oppressor and the man he oppresses at the same time: there remain a dead man and a free man."[31] The armed peasant ushers in a crushing, cataclysmic violence that, along with the destruction of the old regime, brings the nation, liberty, citizens, and men into being.

According to Sartre, justified political violence must unambiguously disavow past political ideals. New men charged with the task of forming a new polity need a novel political vocabulary. In the colonial context, for instance, the revolutionaries must understand that the European talk of "liberty, equality, fraternity, love, honour, patriotism and what have you" is useless "chatter." They must refuse to define themselves or justify their political violence in these false terms.[32]

The transformative power of revolutionary violence rests in a realization that the ideals of the regime in power are a farce. These principles are "nothing but an ideology of lies, a perfect justification for pillage; its honeyed words, its affectation of sensibility [are] only alibis for . . . aggression." True revolutionaries, using violence as a cleansing force, reject these seductive words and ideas just as they embrace a new political world. "[W]ide-awake" to the falsehoods of those in power, they understand that "we only become what we are by the radical and deep-seated refusal of that which others have made of us."[33]

[30] Sartre, "Preface," emphasis original, 21–22.

[31] Thus, violence, when used correctly, is not only an instrument of death but also a cure of "neurosis" and a "proof of . . . humanity." Sartre, ibid. It is important to note that violence can, according to Sartre, not only make new men but better men. "The child of violence, at every moment he draws from it his humanity. We were men at his expense, he makes himself a man at ours: a different man, of higher quality" (24).

[32] Ibid., 26.

[33] Ibid., 25, 12, 17.

In its focus on the internal transformative power of bloodshed and its laudatory view of violence, Sartre's theory of violence is singular. Like earlier modern theorists who defended the right of revolution, Sartre examines the potential of those at the bottom to induce significant political change but he also takes this approach further. Rather than treating the masses as an impermeable collective entity, Sartre peers into the psyche of the revolutionary individual and argues that the liberating effects of violence are most deeply felt at an internal, intersubjective level. His approach, it might be said, is to look at violence fomented by the masses from the vantage point of the individual amid the masses. His work examines violence from the bottom and within the bottom.

In its justification for violence, however, Sartre's work continues a longer, more established line of modern political thought beginning with Marx. The rationale for using violence, according to Sartre, lies in the future and in the wholly novel environment that it will produce. The revolutionary, articulating the aim of the violence, argues that it will bring forth an unfamiliar, superior political order and conjures a vision of this unconventional regime by calling on political ideals and ideas that are equally foreign. Indeed, it might be said that the revolutionary attempts to develop a new political language to justify violent change.[34] The aim of the violence, its governing rationale, is pointedly not articulated in the "honeyed words" and ideals of the existing regime. Indeed, these terms are, as Sartre puts it, mere chatter. The justification for revolutionary violence is not found in what has been but in what will be.

The orientation of this rationalization toward the new and the unfamiliar has its intellectual roots in Marx.[35] Defining communism in simple terms as a "revolutionary movement against the existing social and political order," Marx argued that violence might be a necessary mechanism to usher in a new political regime. In Marx's *Communist Manifesto*, then, one finds a theoretical precursor to many of the motifs in Sartre's theory: The older order is repudiated, a new order is envisioned, and violence is justified in the terms of this new order. Like Sartre's armed rebel who has an ear for the seductive, false language of those in power, Marx's proletarian is capable of discerning bourgeois prejudices within mainstream, pacifying talk of law, morality, and religion. With an awareness of this "bourgeois clap-trap," the revolutionary class is able "to cut up, root and branch, the old order of society."[36]

[34] Sartre, for instance, suggests that Fanon speaks in a new language, one exclusively for the colonized. Fanon, though he writes in French, "bends that language to new requirements, makes use of it, and speaks it to the colonized only." Ibid., 10.

[35] Sartre's debt to Marx is at times more overt. Sartre urges, "Natives of all underdeveloped countries, unite!" Ibid., 10.

[36] Marx and Engels, *Karl Marx, Frederick Engels*, 6:519, 502, 508.

Rejecting the authority of bourgeois values, the proletariat embraces a vision of a fundamentally new economic, social, and political order, one with a transformed notion of property, labor, the family, gender, class, and the nation. This vision encompasses "the most radical rupture with traditional property relations; no wonder that its development involved the most radical rupture with traditional ideas." The political goal of attaining this radical vision requires radical methods; specifically, it "can be attained only by the forcible overthrow of all existing social conditions," by a "violent overthrow of the bourgeoisie [that] lays the foundation for the sway of the proletariat."[37] Violence is a method of achieving this cataclysmic political change—it is "the midwife of every old society pregnant with a new one"[38]—and is justified in terms of a political tomorrow. For Marx, violence for its own sake is neither justified nor productive. Rather, political violence is valid if it serves two ends: to sweep away the old and usher in the new.

Marx's intimation that violence might effectively erase the existing political order was picked up and articulated more forcefully by Bakunin in his discussion of the role of violence in anarchistic struggles. Bakunin firmly ties the will to destroy with the will to create. One needs the other—that is, the effectiveness of violence to destroy the existing society is related to the intensity and power of the vision of the new society. As Bakunin puts it,

> [N]o one can aim at destruction without having at least a remote conception, whether true or false, of the new order which should succeed the one now existing; the more vividly that future is visualized, the more powerful is the force of destruction. . . . For destructive action is ever determined—not only by its essence and the degree of its intensity, but likewise the means used by it—by the positive ideal which constitutes its initial inspiration, its soul.[39]

For Bakunin, the idea of a new political order that prompts the violence need not be true, but it must be deeply, passionately believed. Denied this "positive ideal," the violence loses "its soul." A similar insistence on the necessity of a guiding vision is found in Sorel's *Reflections on Violence*. Sorel, arguing that socialist workers "need not be ashamed of violence," also urged his comrades to "raise themselves above our frivolous society and make themselves worthy of pointing out new roads to the world." According to Sorel, if socialists wished to do something other than act as "servile pupils of [the] detestable past," they must utterly reject middle-

[37] Ibid., 6:504, 519, 495.
[38] Marx, *Capital*, 824.
[39] Bakunin, *Political Philosophy of Bakunin*, 381.

class, statist values, including the notion of the primordial rights of man, and embrace their own, self-constituted mythic vision.[40]

The specific political ends that rationalize the violence vary among Sorel, Bakunin, Marx, and Sartre, and they certainly were not addressing the same political audience. Sorel addressed socialists, Bakunin wrote for anarchists, Marx hoped to inspire communists, and Sartre championed colonial revolutionaries. The substance of their theories and the specific justifications for violence differ. The shape of their arguments, however, is similar. For each, violence initiates a beginning.[41] What's more, violence should indicate a complete disavowal of the existing government as well as the presence of irreconcilable visions of just political rule. These are uncompromising death struggles, in other words, over different conceptions of the good.

This theoretical tradition is clearly at odds with American uncivil disobedience. One might imagine Sartre's disdain for the half measures of the militia movement, his unfavorable assessment of the complicity of the militant abolitionists, and his disapproval of Malcolm X succumbing to the American "chatter" about liberty and self-determination. It is especially important to note that Sartre's radical notion of violence as creative and generative has no audience among members of the militia movement. When McVeigh loaded a Ryder truck with five thousand pounds of ammonium nitrate and nitro methane, for instance, "the old myths" did not "grow dim" and "the prohibitions" were not "one by one forgotten." Just the opposite occurred. For McVeigh, the old myths about American liberty, rights, limited government, citizenship, and democracy grew stronger. And, if, following Sartre, we suggested to McVeigh that he was mistakenly seduced by the "honeyed words" of the dominant regime, we can imagine *his* disdainful response. The fact that Sartre's theory fails to capture the American experience of uncivil disobedience suggests, of course, that we should look elsewhere to understand what is at stake in uncivil disobedience.

Locke's Conventional Revolutionaries

Locke's theory, I have suggested, provides a better lens for deciphering the justifications for uncivil disobedience, as well as a deeper understanding of its significance. Because the extent and nature of Locke's influence on American political thought has been hotly debated, it is important to tread

[40] Sorel, *Reflections on Violence*, 35, 281, 34.

[41] On the problems of conceiving of violence as transformative and creative, see Arendt, "Introduction," in *On Revolution*; and "On Violence" in *Crises of the Republic*.

cautiously here.[42] To be clear, I do not consider the question as to whether uncivil disobedients are directly indebted to Locke (and to no one else). My point is more modest. Locke's theory helps elucidate key aspects of how American uncivil disobedients justify violence and clarifies an important aspect of this violence—that it is a struggle over political legitimacy and the proper place of political power. But, it is important to note that Locke's theory does not address a key issue raised by uncivil disobedience, a point addressed in the final section of this chapter. This lingering question about resistance that results in injustices rightly suggests that a theory written in late seventeenth-century England is limited in what it can reveal about American politics. Locke's theory provides an excellent theoretical lens for examining uncivil disobedience, but it is still a lens. It illuminates some aspects well and occludes others.

At the end of the Second Treatise, Locke famously considered the legitimacy of a revolutionary struggle against a tyrannical prince or a legislature that acts contrary to the trust established with the people. Compared to Sartre's revolutionary peasants, Locke's revolutionaries are unabashedly retrospective. They look to the past, for instance, to understand what is wrong with their present condition. Locke's revolutionaries are prompted to act by a yawning gap between the "original agreement" that bound the people and their government together. This trust, as Locke often refers to it, has become attenuated to the point that government officials are a hostile force, "arbitrary disposers of the lives, liberties, or fortunes of the people." With this, government officials "untie the knot." The original, shared bond that attached the people to the government unravels. For the revolutionaries, the laws and institutions that once seemed close and recognizable have an alien quality. As they see it, the government has become like the "captain of the ship . . . carrying him and the rest of the company to Algiers" and is bent on enslaving them.[43]

A revolutionary faction's perception that the original agreement has been violated does not ensure success, however. Merely having a valid complaint is not enough. Locke is careful to point out that some revolutionary factions will fail because they are unable to persuade a majority of the people that significant political harm has occurred. In such cases, the violation remains "private." Violence against the government may still be justified in the case of a private violation; the harmed group still has the right to defend itself and to recover by force what was wrongfully taken from it. Still, Locke is clear that a private violation will not initiate a successful revolution. Indeed, Locke suggests the opposite. As Locke

[42] See, for instance, Hartz, *Liberal Tradition in America*; Smith, *Civic Ideals*; Young, *Reconsidering American Liberalism*.

[43] John Locke, *Two Treatises of Government*, pars. 243, 221, 227, 210.

unequivocally puts it, individuals fighting the government in the name of a private violation "are sure to perish."[44]

To succeed, the revolutionaries must get the people to reexamine the original agreement and see that the government has violated it. The people must look to the past and then see the current government at odds with the trust they placed in it. In these cases, the government's violation rises beyond the private concerns of the group and extends beyond contemporaneous concerns. The violation becomes political. Like the revolutionary faction, the people need to be prompted to see that the government has violated their "original liberty." Framed in terms of loss and violation, the Lockean revolution is prompted by a remembrance of a "power given with trust for the attaining an end" and an anger at a government "so foolish, or so wicked, as to lay and carry on designs against the liberties and properties" of its subjects. The idea of violation, in other words, is comprehended through a recollection of the dictates of the original agreement, that is, the "fiduciary power" extended to government to "act for certain ends."[45] Locke understands a successful revolution in a way that references the classical understanding of the term and touches on modern sensibilities. As it was for the ancients, a successful revolution for Locke requires a return to an earlier condition; it entails circling back to the beginning. Yet, in the Second Treatise, this return is mental not physical. The people remember what the agreement was about, why it came it to being, and its purpose.[46] They do not, Locke is careful to point out, actually return to the physical condition, the state of nature, that prompted the formation of the agreement with government. They do hark back to this earlier period in their minds, adopting it as a vantage point on the contemporary political situation.

If the past agreement does seem at odds with the present government, an intriguing flip occurs: The government is perceived as the rebel rather than the faction itself.[47] In this political magic trick, a good government disappears and a corrupt regime stands in its place. Thus, a once legitimate government will look like nothing more than "a thief and a robber"

[44] Ibid. par. 208.

[45] Ibid. pars. 222 and 149.

[46] The successful revolutionary faction will make a plausible argument that the power put in the hands of the government for "the preservation of their properties, [has been] applied to other ends, and made use of to impoverish, harass, or subdue [the people] to the arbitrary and irregular commands of those that have it." Ibid., par. 201. On the social contract as a trust, see pars. 222, 226–27. Also see Laslett's introduction (pp. 113–17).

[47] The proper ends of government, according to Locke, concern the protection of property. The people "choose and authorize a legislative" to make laws and rules, which are "guards and fences to the properties of all the members of society." If the government transgresses "this fundamental rule of society," it forfeits the power "people had put into their hands, for quite contrary ends." Ibid., par. 222.

who "may be opposed, as any other man, who by force invades the right of another."[48] The laws of this government will be emptied of legitimacy. Rather than being informed by the ideals and limits specified in the trust with government, these laws look more like arbitrary impositions of an alien, unfamiliar, and illegitimate regime.[49] The magician performing this trick is the revolutionary faction. By showing greater reverence to the social contract, it has more credibility than the government.

The struggle over who can legitimately lay claim to better understanding the original social contract does not imply an ambiguous or open-ended conflict. For Locke, there will be a clear winner and loser. The combatants may be fighting over a shared notion of legitimacy, but, as Locke understands it, legitimate power itself cannot be shared. Legitimacy must reside with the government or the people. The supreme, legitimate power to rule, as Locke points out repeatedly, cannot exist in two locations at the same time.[50] If the government loses legitimate power through a revolution, then it reverts to the people collectively who can do one of three things with it. They can keep legitimate power, continuing "the legislative in themselves"; they can erect a new form of government altogether; or they can place the old social contract "in new hands."[51] Again, in these three options Locke stresses that supreme legitimate power has only one location, either in the hands of the people or in the government.

In contrast with Sartre's revolution, which concerns the nature of legitimate political power, a Lockean revolution is primarily focused on the locus of legitimacy. Just as the people do not physically return to a state of nature when they successfully overthrow a corrupt government, they do not consider anew the question of what constitutes a legitimate political power. The slate of political legitimacy is never truly blank. The central issue, rather, is: Does the government still possess legitimate power or has it been emptied of the rightful power to govern? The combatants in a

[48] Ibid., par. 202.

[49] The importance of revolutionaries to articulate their arguments in terms of the past is also emphasized in Locke's suggestion that a rogue government is like a slave ship on its way to Algiers. In a revolution it will be clear to a normally dutiful and passive subject that the "captain of the Ship . . . was carrying him, and the rest of the company to Algiers," and that his previously trusted government has "steadily returned . . . as soon as the wind and weather, and other circumstances" would allow to a course of enslaving the people (ibid., par. 210). As Locke's nautical metaphor suggests, the revolutionaries' allegation should be that the government has strayed from its proper course. Their charge against government and the rationalization of their violence are framed in terms of the established ends of government and the agreed-upon importance of popular consent to these ends—that is, the initially agreed-upon course.

[50] Ibid. pars. 136, 149, 243.

[51] Ibid., par. 243. Also see Locke's discussion of the formation of civil society. Here Locke also refers to the transfer of legitimate power from individuals to the collective as being definitive and irrevocable.

Lockean revolution battle over a similar notion of political legitimacy; a Lockean revolution is a contest over basically the same notion of the good. Like two dogs fighting over the same bone, the warring parties appeal to the same standard of judgment to attack the other and to defend their own position.[52] Compared to Sartre's theory, Locke's revolution has a claustrophobic quality. It occurs within an enclosed realm of political standards and ideas and it lacks the outside, external perspective of Sartre's revolutionaries who strive to see the political world in an entirely new way.

A Remaining Question

Locke's portrayal of a backward-looking revolution that revolves around a single notion of legitimacy suggests several intriguing insights about uncivil disobedience. First, Locke's theory suggests that uncivil disobedience is, in part, a struggle to gain political legitimacy and to move power into the hands of the citizenry. Also, Locke's theory sorts out the riddle of the backward-looking character of uncivil disobedients' justifications for violence. These retrospective justifications suggest that, like Lockean revolutionaries, uncivil disobedients are fighting for control over a single spoil: political legitimacy.

Thus, when the militia movement rages against the government that has violated the Constitution and asserts that citizens understand the Second Amendment better than the Supreme Court, it attempts to shift legitimate power to the citizenry. The same might be said of southern lynch mobs or western vigilance committees. The mob that broke into the local jail, fought the sheriff for control of the prisoner, and then tried and punished the prisoner was in part attempting to assert the legitimate dominance of the citizenry over established legal institutions. These are instances of resistance to political and legal institutions that attempt to siphon off a degree of their legitimacy, in other words. This draining of legitimacy is never complete, as in a Lockean revolution. Indeed, it might not be successful at all. Still, the aims are similar. The differences between Locke's revolutionaries and uncivil disobedients in this respect are in degree, not in kind. Locke seems to have understood that violence after the establishment of a social contract would very likely be about the provisions, the limitations, and the meaning of the contract. The close of the Second Treatise rightly suggests, then, that the social contract can potentially have a stultifying effect on political imagination. Those who think

[52] We can imagine, for instance, that, in an effort to influence the majority, each side would refer to the initial social contract, the agreed-upon ends of government, the original liberties that government is bound to protect, and the ends and limits of prerogative.

in terms of the Lockean social contract may well be forever looking over their shoulders.

As enlightening as Locke's theory is, however, it is limited in what it can reveal about the possibilities and risks raised by uncivil disobedience. In part, Locke's theory is limited because it makes assumptions about the virtue and passivity of the people that are not borne out by American history. Locke, for instance, assumes that the people are a conservative political force who will resist government only in the most egregious cases. As he famously put it, "People are not so easily got out of their old forms, as some are apt to suggest. They are hardly to be prevailed with to amend acknowledged faults, in the frame they have been accustomed to."[53] In part because of the people's caution, revolution for Locke was a virtuous undertaking. The people, Locke assured his readers, would act rarely and only with good cause. As Locke depicted them, revolutionaries were upstanding, pacific individuals driven to extreme measures by circumstances beyond their control. They were not obstreperous rowdies with a chip on their shoulder. When they did resort to violence, the results were decisive: Either the revolutionaries won and took legitimacy away from the government completely, or they lost, leaving the government in power. This decisive nature of the battle also underscores the revolutionaries' virtue. In Locke's hands, revolutionaries do not muddy the waters of legitimate power. Regardless of whether they won or lost, legitimate power remained a coherent, unambiguous entity. The fight was a fair one, in other words.

Locke's assumptions make sense, of course, given that he was writing about revolution in seventeenth-century England not uncivil disobedience in America. Still, these assumptions limit what his theory reveals about scrambling, intermittent fits of violent dissent throughout American history. Uncivil disobedience has been more frequent and less dramatic than revolution; it suggests a struggle over a more fluid sort of legitimate political power. Challenges to legitimate power in America have been messier and more frequent than Locke's theory would lead one to believe. Instead of a power that decisively shifts from people to government and back, legitimacy in the United States has been subjected to multiple claims and challenges. The fights over legitimacy have been more frequent, less consequential, and not always fair.

[53] Ibid., par. 223. Locke goes on to note that, even when the people do take revolutionary action, the old forms and institutions have a significant grip on their political imaginations. Even in revolution, the people are conservative. In England, Locke observed, the revolutions have tended to "keep us to" the established political structure of the king, the Lords, and the Commons. The king in power may lose his head in a revolution, as Charles I did, and brief political experiments may ensue, as in the interregnum. Still, Locke pointed out, the English had not substantially changed the kind of regime they lived in. See ibid., par. 223.

The history of disobedience in America also indicates a more activist and engaged notion of citizenship than Locke imagined. When Americans have faced an injustice perpetrated by government, they have not been reticent or slow to act. Uncivil disobedients think of themselves as democratic citizens, not subjects, in other words. And, as citizens, they understand that they should be able to assume a direct role in the life and law of the polity. In some cases, they have acted in the name of an injustice that from a Lockean perspective seems insignificant or unworthy of violent resistance. In other cases, uncivil disobedients have not waited for a long train of abuses to develop; they have preemptively struck against what might be the first sign of a *possible* train of abuse. In still other instances, the government's treachery was imagined rather than actual.

The difference between Locke's theory and violent resistance in the United States underscores an outstanding question about uncivil disobedients: Why do they lack the virtue of Locke's imagined revolutionaries? More to the point, why has uncivil disobedience resulted in indiscriminate violence? The history of uncivil disobedience is not just marginally different from Locke's theory on this score. It is markedly different. While Lockean revolutionaries further justice, uncivil disobedients have furthered injustice through random killing. Uncivil disobedience, for instance, has often gone hand in hand with racial and ethnic prejudice and killings and has devolved into what today might be called "hate crimes." Unlike Locke's revolution in which the people are described in undifferentiated and holistic terms, uncivil disobedience has tended to divide the population into racial or ethnic insiders and outsiders. And, outsiders have been killed with little or no provocation. Southern lynching is the paradigmatic example of this tendency, though there are other examples as well: Vigilantes on the frontier hung non whites more readily than whites, armed mobs in the Ozarks attacked homesteaders who did not sufficiently fit in with the community, and John Brown killed pro-slavery outsiders in Pottawatomie Creek, Kansas. Malcolm X tapped into a similarly exclusivist tendency by justifying violence in racial terms and by advocating political empowerment through racial separation. Given this history, the inclination of parts of the militia movement toward racism and anti-Semitism does not appear to be an aberration. Rather, it is indicative of a tendency among uncivil disobedients to divide the citizenry, embrace the homogeneity of insiders, and legitimate violence against outsiders.

Locke's theory also suggests that violent resistance will be directed solely at the government. His virtuous revolutionaries understand that an illicit government is their only enemy. Indeed, even when Locke considered those who have a private violation and are doomed to fail in fomenting a successful revolution, he did not contemplate that violence might be directed at citizens. Locke emphasized the tragic nature of his kind of resistance: the group has a legitimate gripe but the people do not care. He did not, it seems, consider that this type of group might attempt to make the people care by turning the violence toward them too. Yet, here again history parts with theory. Uncivil disobedients have stooped to this level. Sometimes their primary target has been the government, and citizens have been secondary. Other times the reverse has been true. Either way, their violence might be understood as an odd amalgamation of Locke's justified revolution, in which individuals direct their violence at the government for violating the trust, and his state of nature, in which individuals direct their violence at other individuals for violating the law of nature.

Why, then, has uncivil disobedience resulted in such profound injustices? This is a noteworthy question if, following Locke, we believe that revolutions can be virtuous, and, more to the point, we believe that resistance that falls short of revolution—like civil disobedience and strikes—can also be virtuous. Given this position, it seems important to ask how resistance can turn deadly and xenophobic. In particular, what is distinctive about the way uncivil disobedients understand law, popular sovereignty, and the relationship between citizens and government? Both Sartre and Locke contend that the political theory of a resistant group matters. A group's ideas about politics, its struggle, and its relationship with the existing regime shape its goals and what it understands are acceptable methods of resistance. The importance of political ideas in shaping resistance suggests that one way to understand why uncivil disobedients become uncivil is to look more closely at the way they see the political world.

American history can be a great ally in addressing this question. The most prolific uncivil disobedients have left a wealth of information about their normative conception of politics and law. These groups typically record more than their justifications for violence. Some have addressed a wide range of theoretical issues concerning the source of the law, the nature of popular sovereignty, the ideal role of legal officials, and the duty of citizens in a republic. Delving into the political theory of uncivil disobedients is tricky, of course. As I suggested at the beginning of this chapter, there is no reason to uncritically accept everything that uncivil disobedients say. Still, by engaging their ideas critically—not as an adherent or apologist—it is possible to determine how resistance can become reprehensible. The next chapter takes up this task.

Chapter Two

FRONTIER VIGILANCE COMMITTEES

FRONTIER VIGILANTISM IS PUZZLING. On the one hand, the hundreds of vigilante groups that formed on the American western frontier from the first mad days of the gold rush to the end of the nineteenth century seem akin to civil disobedients in the civil rights movement. Frontier vigilantes were impelled to act by a disjuncture between law and morality. Faced with what they thought was an unjust enforcement of the law, vigilantes argued that they were not obligated to obey. Indeed, their defiant actions suggest that they would have agreed with Martin Luther King Jr.'s declaration that citizens may have "a moral responsibility to disobey unjust laws."[1]

Yet, in contrast to civil disobedients, the results of frontier vigilantism were strikingly different. In the worst cases, frontier vigilantes killed people who were innocent of wrongdoing. What's more, like many of their fellow nineteenth-century Americans (and like portions of the militia movement), western vigilantes aspired to a unitary or *herrenvolk* form of self-governance that united individuals through their racial and national identity.[2] Western vigilantes were typically spurred to action by an alleged crime against whites: In cases where the race of the accuser was identified, approximately 90 percent were white. In about half of the cases, the victim was nonwhite.[3] These statistics bear out the general tenor of vigilantism as well. Vigilantes valued homogeneity over difference; they tended toward exclusion rather than inclusion.

A key difference between frontier vigilantes and civil disobedients in the civil rights movement lies in the way each conceptualized the role of citizens in the law. These divergent conceptions enabled some forms of action, foreclosed others, and more generally shaped the conditions in which political action made sense. Frontier vigilantes believed in a peculiar sort of extralegal popular sovereignty in which the people were

[1] King, *Why We Can't Wait*, 82. Also see "The Obligation to Disobey" in Walzer, *Obligations*, 3–23. On the relationship between civil disobedience and violence, see Murphy, *Civil Disobedience and Violence*; Wolff, "On Violence"; and Zinn, *Disobedience and Democracy*.

[2] On the connections between democracy and vigilantism, see Gordon, *Great Arizona Orphan Abduction*, 254–74; Hine, *American West*, 300–315.

[3] Johnson, "Vigilance and the Law." Also see Gordon, *Great Arizona Orphan Abduction*, 262–74; Lamar, *New Encyclopedia of the American West*, 1170; Phillips and Axelrod, *Encyclopedia of the American West*, 1688–96.

legally empowered to suspend law and temporarily change how the law was adjudicated and enforced. Reasoning that the people should be able to see their homogeneous will reflected accurately in every iteration of law, they argued that normal legal officials and institutions could be halted if they diverged from the will of the popular sovereign. In contrast, activists in the civil rights movement conceived of the role of citizens in the law more modestly and in more pluralistic terms. Civil disobedients pointedly did not challenge or supersede the authority of government officials who were charged with enforcing or adjudicating law. They left sheriffs, jailors, and judges untouched, as well as the legal rules that gave these officials the authority to act. While disobedients in the civil rights movement certainly were critical of legal officials, they did not imagine that the people were empowered to suspend the legal order.

Popular Tribunals

The best introduction to how frontier vigilantes conceptualized the law is their own words and actions. There are, fortunately, hundreds of primary documents—including newspaper editorials, speeches, books, manifestos, constitutions, broadsides, diaries, memoirs, and letters—that either describe frontier vigilantism or defend its legitimacy.[4] These give insight into, first, how spontaneous popular tribunals could be understood as a legitimate mechanism to correct the flawed (yet necessary) process of delegating power to legal officials. Second, these documents lend clarity into how frontier vigilantes could claim—loudly, repeatedly, and presumably with a straight face—to be law-abiding, patriotic citizens who broke the law to save it.[5]

The frontier was an odd context, to be sure, filled with legal peculiarities. Foremost, the vast, open space of the frontier had the unexpected effect of shrinking the distance between citizens and the law. In part, this effect was produced by several tangible facts of frontier life. By the end of

[4] There were over two hundred vigilante groups on the frontier. Richard Maxwell Brown, the preeminent historian of American vigilantism, documents 326 vigilante groups throughout the United States, with 210 of these occurring in the West. Brown, *Strain of Violence*, 98–103. David Johnson, focusing on *incidents* of vigilantism in the West, documents 380 incidents of vigilante justice between 1849 and 1902. Johnson, "Vigilance and the Law," 560. I selected the following cases because they are representative of the larger set of cases, and they illuminate how frontier vigilantes conceptualized the relationship between citizens and the law. I also looked for cases that were reported in more than one primary document. Though these multiple sources vary on small details, they tell the same general story.

[5] It is possible that vigilante explanations and justifications were a ruse. What appears to be true and authentic may well not be. See Herzog, *Cunning*. But, if so, the ruse was an elaborate one.

the 1850s approximately 180,000 pioneers had rushed into California, which was in no way ready for such an onslaught.[6] There was a palpable lack of political and legal infrastructure.[7] Civic and legal organization was hampered, moreover, by the fact that miners hailed from across the globe and represented a range of ethnic, racial, and religious backgrounds. Sizable contingents arrived from Ireland, Australia, China, Hawaii, France, Germany, and Italy, as well as from the United States. Former slaves, Mexicans, and Native Americans joined the fray as well.[8] Regardless of these challenges, towns needed to be founded, camps had to be created, and legal order needed to be established, all largely without formal state or federal control. Mining law, for instance, was unsettled by the sudden and unprecedented mass of miners inundating the goldfields. The sheer number of miners raised a bevy of unforeseen issues and revealed the inadequacies and omissions of existing mining law and property rights.[9]

Pioneers may have come for gold, in other words, but what they often got were law and politics. Faced with inadequacies, deficiencies, and in some cases just plain lack of law, miners and pioneers acted collectively to address needs as they arose. Miners themselves, for instance, rectified the problems in mining law by developing a set of codes that were honed and tested by their experiences. This so-called California common law was developed largely without professional assistance (only 619 attorneys gained admission to practice law in California in the 1850s).[10] Yet, the law that the miners developed was solid. It was adopted, essentially wholesale, by the Public Lands Commission in the 1880s.[11] A similar can-do legal ethos was apparent on the overland trail. Pioneers heeded

[6] Paul and West, *Mining Frontiers of the Far West*, 200–225; Rohrbough, "No Boy's Play."

[7] On the problems of civic inaction on the frontier and the overland trail, see Royce, *California*; White, "Trashing the Trails."

[8] Taylor, "African American Men in the American West." On national and ethnic tensions on the frontier and among miners, see Sucheng Chan, "A People of Exceptional Character"; Paul and West, *Mining Frontiers of the Far West*, 25–28 and 253–83.

[9] What, for instance, counted as laying claim to an area for exploration? How many claims could an individual make and how much land could a claim cover? How often did the miner have to work on the land to maintain the claim? And, perhaps most importantly, could a miner follow a vein that extended beyond the boundaries of the claim? According to California law, a miner could lawfully pursue a vein regardless of surface markers, yet this too raised questions as to how to determine when a vein had ended. See, for instance, Paul and West, *Mining Frontiers of the Far West*, 22–24. Because existing law did not always address the changing circumstances of the frontier, following the law could result in gross injustices. As the miners themselves put it, strict observation of existing mining regulations gave them "law but not equity." Bancroft, *Works*, 36:629.

[10] Bakken, *Practicing Law in Frontier California*, 2.

[11] Paul and West, *Mining Frontiers of the Far West*, 161–75; Shinn, *Mining Camps*, 232–58.

property rights, even when faced with starvation; they discerned various types of property holding (private, company, and partnership); they negotiated concurrent property holdings, even when there were no attorneys to consult.[12] The frontier demanded competence and self-sufficiency in the law. As one pioneer succinctly put it, "the only law that we had was that formulated unto ourselves."[13]

Yet this can-do legal ethos played out in a contradictory fashion on the frontier around the issue of legal officials. The sheriffs, justices of the peace, alcaldes, and judges who enforced or adjudicated the law were simultaneously disdained and valued. Pioneers and frontier vigilantes were often scornful of legal claims of expertise.[14] Virtuous, public-minded souls (or dim-witted dupes, depending on how one looked at it) who were willing to serve the common good (and to forgo the possibility of inconceivable wealth) were often in short supply. And many were suspicious of anyone eager to be a sheriff, a judge, or a legislator. They argued, often with good reason, that frontier officials were probably just as venal and hedonistic as any other argonaut. Bribery, corruption, and vice were constant concerns. Frontier vigilantes were also unstintingly scornful of due process, seeing legal procedures and "technicalities" as mechanisms that hid deception and dishonesty.[15] "Where the people looked for justice," one apologist for vigilantism noted, "they found too often jokes and jeers. It was not uncommon to see a judge appear upon the bench in a state of intoxication, and make no scruple to attack with fist, cane, or revolver any who offended him." He added, "Courts of law were in bad repute in those days. Venality and corruption sat on the bench in the form of dueling, drinking, fist fighting, and licentious judges." Complaints about law enforcement were common as well. The San Francisco Vigilance Committee of 1851 proclaimed, for instance, "We are determined that no thief, burglar, incendiary, or assassin shall escape punishment either by quibbles of the law, the insecurity of prisons, the carelessness or corruption of police, or a laxity of those who pretend to administer justice."[16]

But, at the same time, avarice made the idea of legal officers appealing. Miners had no desire to be constantly involved in legal and political matters. They may have been able participatory citizens, but they weren't

[12] Reid, *Law for the Elephant*. On the workings and normative conceptions of law prior to the gold rush, see Hamilton, *Anglo-American Law of the Frontier*; and Langum, *Law and Community on the Mexican California Frontier*.

[13] Reid, *Law for the Elephant*, 9. On justifications for killing on the overland trail, see Reid, *Policing the Elephant*, 193–208.

[14] Aron, *How the West Was Lost*, 82–101; Bakken, *Practicing Law in Frontier California*, 124–37.

[15] On vigilantes resistance to due process, see Pfeifer, *Rough Justice*, 94–109. Also see Bancroft's attack on the presumption of innocence. Bancroft, *Works*, 37:688–89.

[16] Bancroft, *Works*, 37:332. *San Francisco Vigilance Committee of '56*, 11.

willing ones. Miners preferred to work hard—some kept exhaustion at bay with shots of bourbon laced with cocaine[17]—and to celebrate hard with drink, gambling, sex, trips to opium dens, and extravagant feasts. Legal officers made this possible. Thus, except for a few exceptional circumstances, most frontier towns and mining camps had a legal officer of some sort. Moreover, contrary to popular perception, frontier vigilantism typically occurred in towns or camps with an officer of the law.[18] Vigilantes rarely acted in the law's complete absence.

These two contradictory impulses—the loathing of officers of the law and courts and a begrudging sense of their necessity—were able to hang in some sort of balance for much of the frontier's history. There were times, however, when the balance fell apart. These moments of disintegration are particularly revealing of vigilante ideas and assumptions about law. Vigilantes reveal how law failed, as they saw it, and explained how law and order could be regenerated through their violence.[19] Consider, for instance, the concept of law revealed during an 1855 instance of frontier vigilantism in Columbia, California. Problems began with a seemingly inconsequential altercation: Martha, the proprietress of Martha's Saloon and Fandango House fought with John H. Smith, a miner, over a broken pitcher.[20] Martha's husband, John S. Barclay, stepped in to defend his wife and killed Smith. Though Barclay was quickly taken into custody by the local authorities, a mob broke into the local jail using crowbars, sledgehammers, and axes in order to judge and punish Barclay themselves.[21] Quickly forming a popular tribunal, the group established Barclay's guilt and set out to kill him, a task that was complicated by a mishap. In their haste, the vigilantes neglected to pin Barclay's arms, and thus he was able to grip the rope above his head and preserve his life for a brief period.

[17] On life in the mining camps, see Johnson, *Roaring Camp*, Limerick, *Something in the Soil*, 215–20; Paul and West, *Mining Frontiers of the Far West*, 200–225. For a revealing portrait of the squalor and disorder of camps, see White, "Trashing the Trails."

[18] Excluding three exceptional situations—the overland journey to the frontier, the very early days of the mining camps, and the settlements in Alaska—law enforcement and adjudication was present on the frontier. On the presence of legal authorities and vigilantism, see Brown, *Strain of Violence*, 123–24; Caughey, *Their Majesties, the Mob*, 8; Gordon, *Great Arizona Orphan Abduction*, 256; Pfeifer, *Rough Justice*, 28–33; Prassel, *Western Peace Officer*, 96 and 129; Ridge, "Disorder, Crime, and Punishment in the California Gold Rush."

[19] Slotkin, *Regeneration through Violence*.

[20] Accounts differ as to just how heated the argument between Smith and Martha was. Bancroft reports that Smith struck Martha while Lang describes the two as exchanging "high words." Dane reports that Smith shoved Martha into a chair. Bancroft, *Works*, 36:548; Dane and Dane, *Ghost Town*, 265; Lang, *History of Tuolumne County*, 191.

[21] The narrative accounts of the case do not give any indication of why the residents felt that legal officials or the legal process was insufficient. There may have been suspicion that Martha would have used her wealth to corrupt the legal process. Or the vigilantes may have feared that a jury would be convinced that Barclay was legitimately defending his wife, as chivalry codes of the day dictated.

Undaunted, the vigilantes jerked Barclay up and down to break his hold and yelled, "Let go, you damned fool, let go!" Barclay's strength eventually gave out; he did let go.

The killing was legitimated, in part, because Barclay was seen as dissipated and debauched. Barclay's wife, Martha, not only owned the town saloon, but also was the local prostitute. This fact rendered Barclay morally suspect, because, while frequenting a prostitute was acceptable, marrying one was not.[22] As one of Barclay's critics put it, it was as if "a fellow would buy a church and use it as a stable."[23] The situation was made worse because, in a further inversion of gender roles, Barclay was dependent on Martha's income.[24]

Jim Coffroth, a former California state senator, offered an additional explanation for the legitimacy of Barclay's killing. Coffroth's leadership in the killing and the trial—he acted as the "prosecuting attorney"—gave him a platform to address how a former lawmaker could, in good conscience, participate in an extralegal act of violence. How could anyone, especially a former legislator, legitimately take the law into his or her own hands? Coffroth explained:

> Gentlemen, you have elected me to make laws. Ordinarily I am in favor of sustaining the laws and letting them take their course. But you know and I know, gentlemen . . . that the law doesn't always go straight and sure down its proper course to the ends of justice. And there are extremities, gentlemen . . . when the demands of justice are too great to wait upon the law. You are the people . . . and the power the law has comes from you. When you feel a responsibility too great to trust the law you may take that power into your own hands again.[25]

Coffroth assumes two alternatives. If law as made by legislators like Coffroth or as enforced by the town's sheriff could be "trusted," then so be it. But if "extremities" thwarted the true expression of popular will and led it from "its proper course to the ends of justice," it was up to the sovereign people to correct the situation. It is important to note that, as Cof-

[22] For more on legal regulations of sexual morality on the frontier, see Prassel, *Western Peace Officer,* 19–20.

[23] Dane and Dane, *Ghost Town,* 264.

[24] Martha's economic power was somewhat unusual on the frontier. The frontier, despite its reputation as a fabled land of opportunity, did not lead to significant changes in the amount of social or economic power that white women wielded. Faragher, *Women and Men on the Overland Trail.* Also see Levy, *They Saw the Elephant.* The situation for women of color on the frontier was significantly worse. See Hurtado, *Intimate Frontiers.* For more on the effect of mining on Native American women, see Paul and West, *Mining Frontiers of the Far West,* 202–206; West, *Contested Plains.*

[25] Dane and Dane, *Ghost Town,* 266. Also see Lang, *History of Tuolumne County, California,* 192.

froth conceived it, this correction did not consist of vigilantes engaging in popular legislation or authoring the law anew. Rather, vigilantism consisted of bypassing existing legal institutions and withdrawing the power that had been extended to legal officials. The image that comes to mind is of a spigot: Vigilantes stopped the flow of power to legal institutions. It is tempting to think of this power as prelegal and therefore as foundational of the legal order (or, to put it differently, as the power of a founder). But, as will become clear, that's not exactly how vigilantes thought of it.

Coffroth's explanation of vigilantism as a legitimate expression of popular will in light of a failure of legal officials was echoed across the frontier. The San Francisco Vigilance Committee of 1856 justified its actions in similar terms. The '56 vigilantes "undertook and performed good work. They did no injustice. They did no wrong. They did the duty of good citizens and good citizens approved their course. We do not hesitate to say that they did right, having in view this grand republican principle—the will of good people should be the law of our land."[26] Another vigilante organization proclaimed in its published manifesto, "We are believers in the doctrine of popular sovereignty; that the people of this country are the real sovereigns, and that whenever the laws, made by whom they have delegated their authority, are found inadequate to their protection, it is the right of the people to take the protection of their property into their own hands."[27]

Underlying these justifications for vigilantism as a direct expression of popular will is an assumption about the subservient relationship of government officials to the people. As a legislator, Coffroth explains, he exercised a power that ultimately rested elsewhere ("You are the people . . . and the power the law has comes from you") and that could legitimately be taken from him ("you may take that power into your hands again"). This conception of government officials as designates who were vulnerable to a revocation of their power was oft repeated on the frontier. According to one commentator, the people never gave executive power to government officials for any extended period of time, but rather the "executive has no power except such as is daily and hourly continued to him by the people."[28] Power was merely loaned to the people's official agents for short periods of time and could be revoked when necessary.[29]

To put the point differently, the balance between loathing of and begrudging need for legal officers was maintained so long as a stipulation

[26] *San Francisco Vigilance Committee of '56,* 60. Popular acceptance of capital punishments was also important on the overland trail. Reid, *Policing the Elephant,* 181–92.

[27] Mott, *History of the Regulators of Northern Indiana,* 16.

[28] Bancroft, *Works,* 37:671. For Bancroft, then, vigilantism was not properly understood as taking back of power but rather as a halting of a continuous transfer. As a result, the sovereign power was left to enforce and define the law where it originated, with the people. The power was theirs to give or keep, and vigilantes simply chose the latter.

[29] On the multiple meanings of popular sovereignty in the early American context, see Miller, "Ghostly Body Politic."

was met: Law, as enforced or adjudicated, should reflected the will of the popular sovereign. Legal officials were tolerated with the implicit understanding that they were conduits of popular will, manifesting it through execution and adjudication. Frontier vigilantes tended to think of legal officials as delegates rather than representatives. As Nadia Urbinati has drawn the distinction, delegates preserve "popular sovereignty as a unitary act of will" while representatives do not. Thus, "[d]elegation, unlike representation, means that delegates discuss and deliberate but do not have the last word."[30] As vigilantes understood it, the people always had the last word, no matter who or what had to be interrupted to allow them to speak.

It is important to note that vigilantes and their defenders did not understand these popular interruptions and interventions as outside of the law. Vigilantes typically described what they were doing as responding to an emergency—recall Coffroth's appeal to the "extremities" of the Barclay situation. They understood halting their delegates as a constitutionally legitimate part of the legal and political order that they had founded. It was legal, though clearly outside the law. As one commentator put it, "vigilance becomes omnipotent, not as a usurper, but as a friend in an emergency . . . and if law must be broken to save the state, then it breaks it soberly, conscientiously, and under the formulas of law."[31]

Consider, for instance, the extent to which a group of vigilantes in Jacksonville, Oregon, thought of themselves as embedded in law at the very moment that they arrested its normal procedures. An unfavorable ruling against an amiable and popular miner who had fallen on hard times instigated this incident of vigilantism. Some miners believed that the justice of the peace who issued the decision was bribed, while others thought the ruling was unconscionably harsh. Lacking a court of appeal, the vigilantes fashioned their own tribunal, cheekily calling themselves the Jacksonville Supreme Court. The vigilante court convened, finding both the miner and the justice of the peace guilty. In an unusual turn of events, neither was killed or harmed.

One might not read too much into their chosen name except that it was indicative of a vigilante tendency to conduct themselves as courts of law, albeit unusual ones, and to explain their actions in legal terms. Bear in mind, for instance, how Paine Page Prim, a leader of the Jacksonville vigilantes who went on to become Chief Justice of the Oregon Supreme Court from 1864 to 1866 and again from 1870 to 1872, justified vigilantes superseding the authority of the local justice of the peace.

> [T]he farthest back we can go is to the source of the law, the omnipresent power of the people. That power is here, as indeed it is in every society, the central and cohesive force. . . . Who made this

[30] Urbinati, *Representative Democracy*, 62.
[31] Bancroft, *Works*, 36:10.

> scoundrel judge? The people; and if the people possess the power to appoint one man to hang another, may they not make a court high enough to hang, if need be, another court that they have made? I tell you . . . within twenty-four hours I will have here such a court of appeal as will teach Oregon and the world a lesson throughout all ages—a lesson inscribed in the beginning upon the hearts of men, but which is just now beginning to be read, that ever before all statutes and constitutions is the unwritten law of man.[32]

Though Prim proposed halting the legal order, he simultaneously appeals to the institutions and language of law. The people, he noted, were its rightful source; vigilantism was a "court high enough to hang . . . another court." Prim seems to think of vigilantism as outside of the law at some points ("before all statutes and constitutions") and as comparable to the established legal system at other points (as "a court of appeal" to judge "this scoundrel judge"). Prim's notion that vigilantism was simultaneously connected and separated from the law was echoed in vigilante practices. The Jacksonville vigilantes could have addressed the problem they faced in any number of ways: organizing a citizen convention, petitioning political leaders in the States, holding a public forum, or establishing a new civic association. They chose the complicated endeavor of instituting themselves as a provisional court, replete with a judge, witnesses, a jury, and attorneys for the prosecution and the defense. At the very moment that they refused the established legal order, they embraced its concepts and practices.

Prim also makes an illuminating comment that underscores the extralegal (that is, extra and legal) character of vigilantism. He unites two powers that are typically considered distinct and unrelated when he argues that the power to elect a justice of the peace implies the power to supersede this official's legal authority. The first power is an established power that is ingrained in the normal operations of the existing legal order. This more mundane kind of power is exercised once a political regime has been established and it instigates changes in personnel within that order, altering who makes laws or adjudicates them. As such, it is derivative of the legal order and is indicative that this order is functioning normally. The second power Prim refers to—the power to suspend the law of this order's legitimate official in an emergency and to create an ad hoc popular tribunal—is more expansive and innovative. It alters rules governing how power is conferred and indicates a sovereign endowed with the power to stand outside of the legal order. Creating a popular tribunal in

[32] Ibid. 36:627–28. This case also appears in Shinn, *Mining Camps*, 190–98. The general outline of the accounts is similar, though Shinn refers to Rogers as an alcalde, an elected catch-all office that combined the duties of a justice of the peace, sheriff, mayor, and tax collector. Shinn also refers to the miner as Sim, while Bancroft refers to him as Sims.

Jacksonville not only changed who adjudicated the law, it effectively changed how the law was adjudicated.

On the frontier, the conceptual blurring of established and establishing powers was fairly common. It likely did not draw criticism or even comment in Jacksonville because it was allied with two common assumptions. First, all legal power flowed from the people. As such, the power to elect legal officials could imply the power to halt rules governing how power was conferred. If the people could elect officials in its sovereign capacity, then, as vigilantes saw it, it clearly also had the sovereign power to suspend these officials from acting. Since both powers were demonstrations of sovereignty, one could imply the other. Sovereign power was associated with constituted and constituting powers, in other words, and no sharp distinction between the two was perceived. Second, vigilantes believed the legal order was capacious enough to include mundane events like running elections, hammering out legislation, and issuing legal rulings, as well as special moments of intervention by the sovereign people. As they saw it, the sphere of the legal order was considerable, taking in the ordinary and the extraordinary.

One final and central element of Prim's justification stands in need of exploration. As many frontier vigilantes did, Prim refers to the "the people" as the source of the law, a reference that generally did not attract much interest, let alone consternation. Indeed, both defenders of vigilantism and critics tended to understand the practice as an expression of the specific and cohesive will of "the people" or "the community." Yet, who is the "people" or the "community" in these references? Who gets to say what constitutes the will of the people and what justifies their saying it? These are questions about which frontier vigilantes (and, more notably, their nineteenth-century critics) were silent.

This silence suggests that the process of how to form a people was not a central concern. To the extent that the people were constituted, it seems to have been after the fact—that is, the violence of vigilantism itself constituted political membership, rather than a previously defined "people" expressing itself through vigilantism. Concerted violent action brought the people into being, giving form and substance to what was an abstract metaphysical idea.[33] As Franz Fanon noted, the practice of collective violence has the capacity to bind individuals "together as a whole," each one "a link in the great chain, a part of the great organism of violence."[34] On

[33] As Austin Sarat notes of capital punishment, the abstract quality of popular sovereignty may be related to concrete and violent action: "Where sovereignty is most fragile, as it always is where its locus is in 'the People,' dramatic symbols of its presence, like capital punishment, may be most important." Sarat, "Capital Punishment as Legal, Political, and Cultural Fact."

[34] Fanon, *Wretched of the Earth*, 93. Also see Arendt, "On Violence," 163–68. As Timothy Kaufman-Osborn points out, the practices and forms of punishment can be a useful means to interrogate an underlying conception of power. Kaufman-Osborn, *From Noose to Needle*.

the frontier, the cohesiveness of this violent community was strengthened by the fact that, in acting together, culpability for the victim's death was obscured. Like Russian peasant women who in the early 1900s reportedly killed horse thieves by thrusting needles and pins into the victim until death ensued, the Mau-Mau of Kenya who compelled each member of the group to strike a blow at the victim, or the modern firing squad, which shoots the victim together, vigilantes made efforts to spread broadly responsibility for killing.[35] If the victim was hung, vigilantes typically held the rope together. As such each individual was personally responsible for the victim's death and no one was. The "people" had acted.

Vigilantes are best understood both as a product of ambiguity about who could properly speak for the people and as an attempt to eschew this uncertainty. Did officials and representatives always represent the will of the people? Cleverly (and perhaps unwittingly) using the uncertainty of popular will in a representative scheme of government to their best advantage, vigilantes pointed to themselves as the embodiment of the will of the people. It is important to note that there was an empirical logic to their claim to speak for the community. They could identify themselves as the nominal embodiment of the people and in a way that legal officials, as the embodiment of law, could not. The town sheriff guarding the prisoner from vigilantes could not as clearly identify the popular sovereignty that justified his acts, especially when the crowd of vigilantes in front of him claimed otherwise. At the same time that frontier vigilantes used this ambiguity about popular sovereignty to boost their own legitimacy, they denied that popular sovereignty was actually indistinct. For them, popular will was not a ghostly concept, endowed with a shifting nature and blurry borders. It existed; they were it. By their own estimation, they did have more democratic legitimacy than the sheriff or deputy. They *were* the people.

An important implication of believing in a naturalized organic sovereign people was that frontier vigilantes did not tolerate internal dissent. Or, to put it more precisely, they idealized action that was free from the appearance of disagreement and opposition. Attorneys for the defense were shouted down;[36] juries that reached a verdict of innocence were sent back to deliberate some more;[37] and legal officials who opposed vigilantes were threatened with violence. Frontier vigilantes strove to speak with one voice, to articulate one will. As the San Francisco Vigilance Committee of 1851 put it: "Be of one mind, and carry your point. The might, majesty, and power of the people can overcome all impending evils; like the thunders of heaven it will shake to naught all corruptive

[35] On the punishment of horse thieves in Russia, see Cutler, *Lynch-Law*, 3. On the Mau-Mau of Kenya, see Fanon, *Wretched of the Earth*, 85.

[36] Bancroft, *Works*, 36:547–53; Dane and Dane, *Ghost Town*, 265–75; Lang, *History of Tuolumne County, California*, 190–97.

[37] King, *Mountaineering in the Sierra Nevada*, 308–313.

influences and drive its authors into oblivion." Emphasizing a similar point, the 1856 San Francisco Vigilance Committee's constitution held:

> That the action of this body shall be entirely and vigorously free from all consideration of, or participation in the merits or demerits, or opinion or acts, of any or all sects, political parties, or sectional divisions in the community; and every class of orderly citizens, of whatever sect, party, or nativity, may become members of this body. No discussion of political, sectional, or sectarian subjects shall be allowed in the rooms of the association.

The hope was that homogeneity would allow frontier vigilantes to "rise as one man, summoned by almighty conscience."[38] While frontier vigilantes were not particularly concerned with how this "one man" was constituted, they were certain that they had to act as one man, not many individuals. To effectively unite will and law, the people had to have one will, one voice, one conscience, and one desire.[39] As will become clear, this fascination with oneness was a defining trait.

The Rousseauian Legal Dynamic

Vigilantes certainly found themselves in peculiar circumstances on the frontier, but in many ways their motivations were not strange and their expectations about the law not unfamiliar. Vigilantes wanted to make the law respond to justice, they intended to see that justice was done, and they hoped to reassert the rights of the people. For them, even the most minimal, threadbare government was capable of thwarting justice and frustrating popular power. Even in the midst of wilderness, government could become so insensate and remote that it ceased to deliver on the promise of autonomy that legitimated it in the first place. The vigilante response was to reclaim autonomy, recover legitimacy, and repossess the law.

A fruitful place to clarify the longing frontier vigilantes had for a direct unmediated relationship between the people and law is the paradoxical relationship Rousseau described between citizens and the law in the *Social Contract*. Running through the *Social Contract*, on the one hand, is the idea of citizens having direct authorial control over law. Possessing the power to make law that is equivalent to their will, citizens craft laws that

[38] Bancroft, *Works*, 36:460, 37:112–13, 36:16.

[39] Arlene Saxonhouse's observation on the potential risks of unity comes to mind: "[T]he pursuit of unity can create a world that tries to eliminate that which is not easily accommodated into this underlying unity, a world that finds diversity so threatening that it collapses all into one, avoids the multiplicity of human experience, and leaves us immobile and sterile." Saxonhouse, *Fear of Diversity*, x.

are familiar and just. On the other hand, the *Social Contract* describes an institutional arrangement between the sovereign and government that creates disjuncture, fragmentation, and alienation between citizens' will and law. I refer to this conflict as the Rousseauian legal dynamic.

For my purposes, the important aspect of this Rousseauian legal dynamic is the tension it reveals between an active participatory mode of legal engagement and an inactive hands-off mode, between democracy and constitutionalism. The important issue is not whether Rousseau effectively resolves these contradictory positions, creating, as he put it, a "body politic" in which "the words *subject* and *sovereign* are identical correlatives, whose meaning is combined in the single word citizen."[40] Nor is the central point to see whether frontier vigilantes embody this dynamic precisely as Rousseau envisioned it—that is, as self-legislating sovereigns who make the law without the aid of others. They did not. Like most nineteenth-century Americans, frontier vigilantes believed in the legitimacy of legislative representatives, and they were more than willing to delegate legislative responsibilities to others as long as an equivalent relationship between will and law was maintained. What the *Social Contract* lends insight into instead is a tension between radical popular sovereignty that has a direct, immediate control of law and a state of submission to law in which passivity and compliance are key. Frontier vigilantes were enamored with one side of this tension (control of law) and dismissive of the other (submission to law). They were infatuated with democracy and disdainful of constitutionalism.

The first move of the Rousseauian legal dynamic is well understood, but it is worth noting how extensive the popular sovereign's command of the law is. According to the *Social Contract*, the popular sovereign is the only legitimate source of law. Law cannot rightly come from anywhere else. The law, moreover, is only legitimate when it expresses the popular sovereign's universal and collective will. It articulates the inner will and desires of the sovereign, making its wishes, beliefs, and understandings public. Law brings the inside out; it gives the body politic "movement and will." And it is the only means for the popular sovereign to express itself as sovereign: "The sovereign, having no other force than the legislative power, acts only by laws."[41] There is no higher authority on the meaning and intent of the law than the popular sovereign. Even if the people wanted to create a higher legal authority—a supreme court, for instance, of wise judges who could tell them what the law means—it could not. Popular

[40] Rousseau, *On the Social Contract with Geneva Manuscript and Political Economy*, bk. III, chap. 12, 100, emphasis original. Hereafter *S C*.

[41] As Rousseau puts it, "the will of the people as a body . . . is an act of sovereignty and constitutes law." Ibid. bk. II, chap. 2, 59–60; chap. 6, 65; bk. III, chap. 12, 99.

sovereignty, as Rousseau understood it, is inalienable and indivisible. The power to make law belongs exclusively to the people. As such, it is impermeable to modification; it cannot be given away.

At the core of Rousseau's notion of popular sovereignty is an authorial relationship between citizens and law that is remarkably proximate, intimate, and hands-on. The popular sovereign, as the author of the law, gives law life. The law, in turn, reflects the sovereign's will back to it, acting as a record of the sovereign's changing needs and wants. Ideally, the law is a mirror: it reproduces the will of the sovereign back to it by accurately replicating the sovereign's conscious and intentional choices. Like any good mirror, the law must be able to quickly and accurately reproduce changes in the subject that it reflects. As Rousseau succinctly put it, "Yesterday's law does not obligate today." Nor does the law bind the popular sovereign from imprudent action, because, if the sovereign "wishes to do itself harm, who has the right to prevent it from doing so?" The law is inherently protean, and its shape is wholly defined by the will of the popular sovereign.[42] Gaps are unacceptable. Indeed, as Linda Zerilli observes, "the slightest spacing between the citizen-subject and his political voice introduces a momentary noncoincidence that is nothing less than calamitous: 'The general will becomes mute.'"[43]

A chief virtue of the popular sovereign's command over law is that it facilitates the creation of rules that are recognizable and therefore just. No longer the province of authorities that are external and superior to the people (gods and kings), law belongs to the citizenry.[44] As such, Rousseau argued that it was more difficult for laws to be an instrument of repression and injustice. As Rousseau put it, it is "no longer necessary to ask . . . whether the law can be unjust, since no one is unjust to himself; nor how one is free yet subject to the laws, since they merely record our wills."[45]

[42] As Rousseau put it in his much-cited critique of representative legislatures, "Any law that the people in person has not ratified is null; it is not a law. The English people thinks it is free. It greatly deceives itself; it is free only during an election of the members of Parliament. As soon as they are elected, it is a slave, it is nothing." Ibid. bk. III, chap. 15, 102; chap. 11, 99; bk. II, chap. 12, 76.

[43] Zerilli, *Signifying Woman*, 58, quoting Rousseau.

[44] There is an important caveat here: the lawgiver. In chap. 7 of bk. II, Rousseau introduced the lawgiver, a supreme leader who is "capable of changing human nature" and "who can make the Gods speak or be believed when he declares himself to be their interpreter." Rousseau, *S C*, 68, 70. For an argument that the lawgiver does not eliminate the tension between freedom and domination, see Honig, "Between Decision and Deliberation."

[45] Rousseau recognized that the equivalence of the general will and law does not eradicate the possibility that laws might appear unfamiliar, illegitimate, or undesirable to citizens. It is possible, Rousseau admitted, that a citizen's personal interest would clash with the common interest of the law, creating a situation in which obedience to the law seems to violate self-interest and the popular sovereign appears illegitimate (or "an imaginary being"). Rousseau, *S C*, bk. I, chap. 7, 55; bk. II, chap. 6, 66.

Because citizens author law and can identify with it—in short, because the law is an extension of them—it cannot be unjust.

At the same time that Rousseau emphasized the popular sovereign's command over law and identification with it, he also described an institutional arrangement that thwarts its control and, thus, emphasizes the value of constitutionalism. To see this, it is essential to turn to an inviolable restriction placed on the popular sovereign: It is prohibited from enforcing law, as the application and interpretation of the law is the task of the government. While the sovereign reigns supreme in legislating and has the "will" to determine what action will be taken, the government applies the law to specific cases and has the "strength" to set the law in motion.[46] The two institutions have distinct legal roles that cannot be confounded or confused. This bifurcation of power is reflected in the *Social Contract*'s legal terminology as well. The sovereign issues "laws," general rules that consider "the subjects as a body and actions in the abstract, never a man as an individual or a particular action."[47] The government, in contrast, issues "decrees" that apply the law to specific situations and particular individuals.

While Rousseau insists that the sovereign must sit on its hands, refraining from interfering in the government's execution of law, he also acknowledged the difficulty of observing this restraint. How can the creators of the law be silent about its application? What if the government distorts the sovereign's will, transforming what was familiar and just into something that is "uncanny"?[48] According to Rousseau, "He who makes the law knows better than anyone else how it ought to be executed and interpreted," and, thus, it may seem that "there could be no better constitution than one in which the executive power is combined with the legislative."[49]

The need for sovereign restraint is also complicated by the scope of the government's power, which includes, for instance, the power to declare war and to negotiate peace. Far more than a sleepy policeman at the side of the road clocking speeders (though perhaps that too), the government's power is extensive.[50] As Judith Shklar notes, the sovereign "does very little" in comparison.[51] The expansionist character of government, moreover, exacerbates the likelihood that the law will become uncoupled

[46] As Rousseau puts it elsewhere, "[T]he legislative power is the heart of the State, the executive power is its brain, giving movement to all its parts." Underscoring the hierarchical relationship between the sovereign and the government, Rousseau continues: "The brain may become paralyzed, yet the individual is still alive. A man can remain an imbecile and live. But as soon as the heart has ceased to function, the animal is dead." Ibid. bk. III, chap. 11, 99.

[47] Ibid. bk. II, chap. 6, 66. Rousseau goes on: "In short, any function that relates to an individual object does not belong to the legislative power."

[48] Honig, "Between Decision and Deliberation," 5.

[49] Rousseau, *S C*, bk. III, chap. 4, 84.

[50] See, for instance, "On Government" in Johnston, *Encountering Tragedy*, 75–119.

[51] Shklar, *Men and Citizens*, 181.

from sovereign will, and unrecognizable. The nature "of all the governments of the world," Rousseau observed, was to increase their power and "sooner or later usurp the sovereign authority."[52] A logical result might be anxiety about the actual power of the popular sovereign.[53]

Despite the fraught relationship between sovereign and government (or perhaps because of it), Rousseau underscored the necessity of sovereign restraint, insisting that it must maintain a passive, hands-off approach to the interpretation and execution of law. Crossing the boundary between sovereign and government introduces the private interests of legislators on public affairs and "nothing is more dangerous." The polity is irrevocably changed; the result is a "government without a government." Indeed, the *Social Contract* suggests that the very meaning of the law depends on the ability of the sovereign to refrain from acting: "If it were possible for the sovereign to have executive power . . . right and fact would be so completely confounded that one would no longer know what is law and what isn't."[54] For law to be law, then, there must be moments of repose or constitutionalism in which the sovereign is separated from law, alienated from it, and dominated by it.[55]

Seen through the lens of the Rousseauian legal dynamic, frontier vigilantes seemed distinctly ill at ease with separation from law and restraint of action. Rather, they were certain that the popular sovereign could legitimately intercede in the law. They emphasized the controlling, action-oriented, autonomous and democratic nature of the Rousseauian legal dynamic, if you will. And they were animated to act by a kind of anxiety

[52] Rousseau, *S C*, bk III, chap. 18, 106. Stressing the active autonomous side of this paradox, Rousseau described government officials as essentially lackeys of the sovereign people. The virtue of the government is that it is uncreative; it follows orders. Thus, Rousseau, the great democrat, did not care too much about democracy when it came to the government. This institution could be run as a democracy, an aristocracy, or a monarchy. The political structure of the government is insignificant to Rousseau because its only goal is to effectuate the will of the sovereign people. And if the government displeases the sovereign, it can be removed. The sovereign, Rousseau declared, "can limit, modify, and take back" the power that it delegates to the government "whenever it pleases." Ibid., bk. III, chap. 1, 79.

[53] As Steven Johnston notes, "While the centerpiece of a Rousseauian theory might seem to be the preservation of sovereignty from the machinations of government, an ethic of governmentality has already executed a coup d'etat. Thus Rousseau's texts dethrone sovereignty even as they announce its reign." Johnston, *Encountering Tragedy*, 75–77. Also see Rousseau, *S C*, bk. III, chap. 14, on the government's anxiety when the people assemble as a sovereign body.

[54] Rousseau, *S C*, bk. III, chap. 4, 84–85; chap. 16, 104.

[55] Law consists of both freedom and domination in other words. Elizabeth Wingrove's analysis of Rousseau's "paradox of law" is helpful on this point. Wingrove explains this paradox in terms of the transition from a state of nature to a contract. The "*autonomous* man strives to overcome, through the contract, the relationships of domination and submission that are necessary to produce the very context in which his *auto* and his *nomos* become intelligible." Wingrove, *Rousseau's Republican Romance*, 56.

and dread hinted at in Rousseauian legal dynamic's emphasis on repose, domination, and the fragmentation of will and law. For frontier vigilantes, entrusting law to officials was an anxious endeavor filled with uncertainty. As they saw it, the problem with delegating power to officials was not that they would naturally usurp power from the sovereign as the *Social Contract* suggests. Frontier vigilantes were anxious for a more prosaic reason. They simply did not trust that officials would refuse duplicity and resist dishonesty. Some did not. Vigilantes in Virginia City, Montana, strung up their own elected sheriff after they discovered he was running a band of thieves and stealing from the very citizens he was elected to protect.

To put it slightly differently, frontier vigilantes were uncomfortable with maintaining the tension between action and inaction and democracy and constitutionalism at the heart of the Rousseauian legal dynamic. They not only normatively favored one side of this tension, but they seemed eager to displace the messy and uncertain position of being in the middle of it. They lacked an understanding of the contradictory desires of the Rousseauian legal dynamic—that is, the pull of radical popular sovereignty and the desire to bring the law to justice, and the need for repose, restraint, and domination by law. Like a light switch, radical popular sovereignty was either on or off; the people were in power or they weren't; government was legitimate or it wasn't; the law was just or unjust. They thought of politics and law as "either/or" propositions. In contrast, the Rousseauian legal dynamic suggests thinking of law and politics in terms of "and": freedom and domination, justice and injustice, popular sovereignty and government. This is a much trickier proposition. Indeed, it's not entirely clear what such an approach to the law might look like.

Democratic Remainders

Placing frontier vigilantism in a broader context and seeing it as an expression of radical popular sovereignty that aims to dominate law raises the question of just how different frontier vigilantes were from civil disobedients in the civil rights movement. Were the Jacksonville vigilantes, who collectively rejected an unjust ruling by the local justice of the peace in 1852, substantively different from civil disobedients who rejected unjust segregation laws in Birmingham, Alabama, in 1963?

This is an important question because, if we think of frontier vigilantism as unruly, dangerous, and ochlocratic, then perhaps we should describe the popular resistance of the civil rights movement in the same terms. Or, if we believe that civil disobedience is a form of democratic activism worthy of emulation, then perhaps some kinds of frontier vigilantism are as well. To continue to champion Martin Luther King Jr., Rosa Parks, and the numerous ordinary citizens who engaged in sit-ins, stand-ins, pray-ins, marches, and protests—as I think we should—it may be necessary to celebrate frontier vigilantism too, or at least some forms of it.

The two phenomena are closer than has commonly been supposed and a plausible argument of democratic legitimacy can be made for both. Taken together, they complicate universalizing claims about the virtues or vices of citizens stepping outside of law in the name of the law. It is misguided to marshal frontier vigilantism (absent a consideration of the civil rights movement) as evidence of the normative advantage of the rule of law, constitutional constraints, civic repose, or an elitist scheme of representation. Likewise, it is problematic to appeal to the civil rights movement (absent a consideration of frontier vigilantism) as validation of the normative superiority of the rule of the people, autonomy, civic activism, or a participatory theory of democracy. Considered together, these events suggest that self-governance is a risky endeavor. Together they remind us, as Honig puts it, that "the people are always also a multitude, the general will is inhabited by the will of all, the law(giver) is possibly a charlatan."[56] Moreover, taken together, they point to an understanding of the relationship between the rule of law and the rule of the people that emphasizes its complexities, its tensions, and its interwoven interdependent character. The balance between citizens as authors and addressees may shift and change, but it seems questionable that one side of this dynamic should meaningfully displace the other.

The line between these two phenomena may be thin and porous; still there is something to it. There are, for instance, significant differences in how the balance between ruling and being ruled was conceptualized by frontier vigilantes and civil disobedients in the civil rights movement. And, to be more specific, there are noteworthy differences in how comfortable each was with what I have called the Rousseauian legal dynamic, which maintains a tension between democracy and constitutionalism. I've suggested that frontier vigilantes were fundamentally ill at ease with the paradoxical and mutually constitutive relationship between autonomy and domination implied in this dynamic. They preferred eradicating domination by law in favor of a radical popular sovereignty that knows no bounds, and sought the ascendancy of one side of this dynamic to the other. Their idea of political agency, to put the point differently, was free of paradox, inconsistency, and contradiction. And, it is important to note, frontier vigilantes also make the appeal of such a position clear. The allure of the ascendancy of democracy and popular sovereignty is, clearly, not based on the actions that it facilitated and justified, but rather on the

[56] Honig, "Between Decision and Deliberation," 14.

simplicity and populism of its prescription: as frontier vigilantes saw it, radical popular sovereignty and popular control of the law was always and already the key to legitimacy. It is much more difficult, as I have suggested, to think about what politics, in between democracy and constitutionalism and political agency, and conceived within the tension of the Rousseauian legal dynamic, might look like. More to the point, it is not entirely apparent that this idea of political agency could withstand the test of sociological realism. Can the Rousseauian legal dynamic be made flesh, as it were?

Civil disobedients in the civil rights movement were comparatively more at ease with the tension between democracy and constitutionalism, and as such, they were exemplars of a type of political agency that is situated in between these ideals. To see this, it is best to focus on how civil disobedients in the civil rights movement conceived of political action and, in particular, how they thought about disobedience. Martin Luther King Jr. famously argued that a miscarriage of justice could legitimately be protested by collectively disobeying the law in public. Extending Augustine's famous statement that "an unjust law is no law at all" (*non videtur esse lex quae justa non fuerit*), King argued that citizens could legitimately break the law. Yet they must do so "lovingly"—that is, they must willingly accept the prescribed punishment for their crime. By accepting the punishment, the civil disobedient, as King put it, "is in reality expressing the highest respect for the law."[57]

King's idea of a loving form of dissent that violates one law while it upholds another provides a concrete way to think about political action and agency within the Rousseauian legal dynamic. By breaking the law collectively and publicly, civil disobedients, on the one hand, express their affinity for democracy, for radical popular sovereignty, and for autonomy. Their disobedience recognizes the importance of making law respond to justice and of reasserting the rights of the people. Their violation of law is a demonstration of their particular beliefs that are distinct from and antithetical to the government's. By submitting to the laws governing their punishment, on the other hand, civil disobedients bow to the demands of constitutionalism, law, and domination. Their obedience to law recognizes the importance of institutions, legal officials, and passivity. By obeying law, they demonstrate that some of their beliefs are also in accord with the government. They effectively occupy the space between democracy and constitutionalism and inhabit the tension inherent in the Rousseauian legal dynamic. Their conception of political agency might reasonably be called active and passive, hands on and hands off, dominating and dominated. In contrast with the frontier vigilante idea of political agency, it is not one thing or the other but both.

[57] King, *Why We Can't Wait*, 83, 84.

The specific actions of civil disobedients in the civil rights movement provide a concrete example of being active and passive in relation to the law. Consider, for instance, King's arrest in Birmingham. King's hope in the power of the people, his moral outrage at segregation statutes, and his antipathy for racist legal officials in Birmingham led him to violate the law requiring that he have a parade permit. These motivations led him to the street, and they led him and others to seek freedom from law. Yet, this activism, righteousness, and autonomy took a secondary role—though it certainly did not altogether fade—when the police approached with their handcuffs. Though these were still the same morally corrupt legal officials, the time of autonomy from law was over. Law dominated civil disobedients. The immorality of these officials and their disproportionate use of force did not matter. Whether officials came with handcuffs or, as was often the case, with fire hoses, dogs, and billy clubs, civil rights activists were asked by the movement to accept their domination. They submitted. In so doing, they yielded not only to those who embodied the law but to the law itself.

The standard reading of the civil rights movement is that their willingness to accept punishment for their crimes indicated that civil disobedients were different from common criminals. Their lawbreaking was not motivated by personal gain, and it was not done secretly or surreptitiously. I do not mean to suggest that this standard reading is incorrect or fundamentally flawed. There are however additional ways to understand and analyze the concept of a loving violation of law. The Rousseauian legal dynamic with its emphasis on action, restraint, autonomy, and domination provides another way to view a loving violation of law and to think about its significance.

A central implication of being in the midst of the tension between democracy and constitutionalism is that civil disobedients in the civil rights movement conceptualized a more distant and discordant relationship between citizens and law. Though they cared passionately about seeing their morality affirmed by law, civil disobedients did not crave the same sort of one-to-one correspondence between law and will as frontier vigilantes did. The demands of constitutionalism and obedience to the law meant that civil disobedients accepted that parts of the law would not and should not be identical to their will. The point was not that the laws governing their punishment were necessarily just. These too could be discriminatory, either as written or as applied. Nor, as the *Letter from Birmingham Jail* makes clear, was the idea that certain laws should be spared criticism and comment.[58] Obedience to the laws of punishment did encourage accepting that the law, even in its ideal form, would not replicate

[58] Ibid., 82–83.

their will and morality. It diffused moral absolutism and political imperialism, in other words. Yet it is important to note that this conception of law also enabled action, avoiding moral relativism and political paralysis.

Another crucial implication of accepting the demands of constitutionalism was that it encouraged accepting a pluralistic notion of the law. By this, I mean that the civil disobedients tended to believe that the polity consisted of distinct and divergent groups and that the law reflected and negotiated their differences. This pluralistic notion of law accepts, as Waldron puts it, that it "is *normal* for law . . . to make claims that are at odds with the sense of justice of some or many of those who are under its authority."[59] Recall, for instance, the metaphor of the law as a mirror of sovereign will. To the extent that civil disobedients imagined that they could see themselves reflected in the law, there were lots of others reflected there as well: sheriffs, deputies, state legislators, members of Congress, federal and states judges, and so on. An obligation to the laws governing their punishment meant that the law reflected this *official* will as well as their own. The important point is not, I think, that civil disobedients recognized official will as such, but rather that they recognized and respected the will of another more generally. Civil disobedients in the civil rights movement exemplify both the desire for a connection between will and law and, more importantly, an acknowledgement that such a bond can never be complete. They wanted to see themselves in the law, yet knew that others would necessarily be reflected in it too. Perhaps because their legal worldview was constituted from a position of subjection and an absence of political power, civil disobedients understood that the law was constituted by clashes over what should be done and how to do it. Multiple perspectives, moralities, and wills constituted democratic law and politics.[60]

It is tempting to describe political action between democracy and constitutionalism in terms of a different approach to legal procedures. Civil disobedients in the civil rights movement tended to accept procedures while frontier vigilantes were hostile to them. This is certainly true as far as it goes. Frontier vigilantes consistently equated official legal procedures with fraud, distortion, opacity, and just plain sluggishness. As Wyoming vigilantes wryly put it in a bit of doggerel pinned to the body of one of their victims, "Process of law is a trifle slow, So this is the way we have to go, Murders and thieves beware! PEOPLES VERDICT."[61] A popular

[59] Jeremy Waldron, *Law and Disagreement*, 7; "Precommitment and Disagreement."

[60] To borrow from Honig, they were able to "see such perhaps necessary moments of alienation in life under law as welcome gaps that remind[ed] [them] of the insufficiencies of juridical efforts to institute justice or legitimacy without remainder. Honig, "Dead Rights, Live Futures," 794.

[61] Quoted in Pfeifer, *Rough Justice*, 108; and West, *Contested Plains*.

vigilante saying echoes this sentiment: "More justice, less law."[62] This contrasts sharply with the idea of a loving violation of the law.

Yet the distinction based on proceduralism does not quite work because frontier vigilantes had numerous procedures: they held trials, called witnesses to the stand, elected judges, heard from juries, issued public proclamations, developed vigilante constitutions, and so on. They were not opposed to procedures in and of themselves but rather disliked procedures that obfuscated the will of the people or made the will of the people untenable because they gave voice to dissent and difference. In short, procedures that revealed discord and recognized disagreement were problematic, as were those about which the sovereign people might reasonably disagree. Procedures and forms that enabled frontier vigilantes to "rise as one man, summoned by almighty conscience," however, were celebrated. To put this point more broadly, legal procedures and constitutional constraints may be valuable to democratic politics in part because they enable pluralism. Legal procedures and the experiences of domination, repose, and restraint that they imply may not be good in and of themselves. Rather, their virtue may lie in allowing conflict and dissent to surface (even about legal procedures themselves). So doing, legal procedures accustom us to a world marked by clashes between citizens and government and by disagreement between and among citizens. The political community may be stronger for it.

It is not difficult to imagine how the tendency to silence conflicting voices on the frontier also eased the slide toward stringing up the wrong fellow and the disproportionate killing of those who looked or acted differently. Without much to impede it, the interests and perspectives of the vigilantes ballooned and blotted out all others. Their needs became paramount; all other concerns were irrelevant. To put it differently, frontier vigilantes, as a group, were not only capable of oppression and injustice, but also of blinding self-absorption and a steadfast conviction that they were always right. What's more, these tendencies were related. For what was to stop the vigilantes from becoming convinced that they were infallible, when, much like a traditional sovereign, the people could assert their control over every aspect of the law? What could restrain popular power or provoke questions about the justice of its exercise? What, in other words, might inject caution or temperance? In some instances, nothing did.

In one case the opposite occurred—that is, allowing for dissent and conflict among the mob halted collective solipsism and the need to act as one man endowed with one will. Dissenting voices did break through at

[62] Quoted in Gordon, *Great Arizona Orphan Abduction*, 258. On vigilantes' resistance to due process, see Pfeifer, *Rough Justice*, 94–109. Also see Bancroft, *Works*, 37:688–89.

a crucial point in the Jacksonville case. In the "sentencing" phase of the proceeding, the vigilante crowd favored hanging the defendant and the justice of the peace, both of whom had been found guilty. Prim along with a few others argued that the lives of these men should be spared. We can only speculate as to what was said; the historical record does not illuminate the specific arguments that persuaded the mob to listen to the dissenters and to reassess its decision. It is clear, however, that speaking out changed the course of events. The vigilantes reconsidered. As a result, the miner and the justice of the peace walked away unharmed. This change in outcome is certainly significant. Imagine the relief of the two men who escaped a vigilante death sentence. But the underlying change in *thinking* seems equally significant. At least momentarily the Jacksonville vigilantes relinquished their fascination with oneness: one man, one will, one conscience, one law. Content to let the dream of amalgamating into a mighty and terrible being recede, they were tolerant of internal disagreement and at ease with discord.

Chapter Three

SOUTHERN LYNCH MOBS

SOMETIMES THE EVENTS THAT DON'T HAPPEN are as telling as the ones that do. Consider a prevented lynching in Hernando, Mississippi, in 1934, an event that gives insight into the legal and political stakes of public lynchings in the post-Reconstruction South. In Hernando, three African American men in their early twenties were arrested for criminally assaulting a seventeen-year-old girl, charges that stirred talk of a lynching. The authorities were intent on trying the men in a court of law and executing them legally.[1] To do this, however, they had to appease the demands of the hundreds of angry citizens milling outside of the jail where the men were being held.

What did this would-be lynch mob want the legal authorities in Hernando to do? What did it hope for from the law? It's difficult to answer these questions with certainty, but three unusual aspects of the Hernando trial give insight into how the authorities hoped to appease the mob and, conversely, what the mob hoped for from the law. What each wanted, it seemed, was to make the trial as much like a public, mass lynching as possible.

The first unusual aspect of the trial was the involvement of the people. The prosecution made sure that the people played a role in the proceedings by requesting a jury trial.[2] Though the defense was content to enter a guilty plea at the arraignment—a move that favored the prosecution and should have been heartily welcomed by it—the prosecution made an atypical request that a jury issue a verdict on the men's guilt.[3]

The second unusual aspect of the trial was its speed. Within a five-hour span on February 12, the defendants were indicted, tried, convicted, and

[1] The judge in the trial, John R. Kuykendall, explained why Mississippi officials were intent on preventing a lynching: "A lynching at this time would have meant something that this county would have felt for years. There are seven bills pending in congress [*sic*] threatening the thing we hold so dear—the rule of the white man in the south. If we had a lynching today, I believe congress would have passed these bills." "Guardsmen Put Condemned Trio Back into Cells." For more on "legal lynchings" (that is, legal trials conducted under pressure from a lynch mob), see Wright, *Racial Violence in Kentucky*.

[2] "Guardsmen Put Condemned Trio Back into Cells."

[3] Ibid. What's more, the judge in the case made efforts to emphasize that trying the defendants in a court of law was not a slight to the people. "I don't want you people to think that the sheriff or I doubted the citizenship of this county," he told a local reporter.

sentenced to death. The jury was especially quick with its task, returning with a guilty verdict in seven minutes.[4] As the judge put it, the trial was "a mere formality."[5]

The final curious aspect of the legal proceedings concerned the punishment. The Hernando authorities made a remarkable bargain with the victim's father, C. W. Collins: In exchange for preventing the would-be lynch mob from taking matters into their own hands, Collins would be permitted to spring the trap at the hanging. Collins agreed. Addressing the mob, he admitted to his desire for vengeance and noted that he, like the mob, was almost overwhelmed by his passion. Still, Collins stated that he was content to let the court express his moral contempt for the offenders and their crime.[6] If Collins felt that the law could satisfy his need for moral outrage and revenge, then how could those who were less directly affected by it argue differently? Collins's appeal was successful; the trial went forward.[7]

The Hernando case is striking, I think, because it exposes a connection between popular morality and law that seems eminently democratic. The Hernando lynch mob, in essence, wanted the law to be representative of its morality. It wanted the law and legal officials to reflect its values. The crowd's substantive notion of morality was highly objectionable. Still, the lynch mob's idea, in and of itself that there *should* be a connection between popular morality and law, is not clearly objectionable. Indeed, it seems plausible. Imagine the case in more abstract terms. Several hundred citizens who feel strongly that the laws are being enforced inadequately or unjustly take to the streets in an effort to influence the legal process. Fearing that authorities will not faithfully adhere to their moral vision, they protest in an unconventional manner outside of the formal political process. Their protest is successful; some of their demands are met. The authorities, in an implicit recognition of popular sentiment, change their actions so as to adhere more closely to the moral vision of the concerned citizens. Empowered and politically savvy, the citizens win. And, so it seems, does popular government. If the group in the example is the civil rights movement, then the benefits are clear.

[4] Mississippi authorities indicated before the trial that it would be speedy. "Prisoners Move from Hinds Jail with Big Escort."

[5] "Guardsmen Put Condemned Trio Back into Cells."

[6] "Prisoners Move from Hinds Jail with Big Escort"; "Three Negroes Doomed."

[7] Collins successfully derailed the lynch mob, but he did not spring the trap at the hanging. In a strange twist of fate, the sheriff who had agreed to let Collins participate in the executions died. Collins appealed to the attorney general of Mississippi, urging him to adhere to the original agreement. His appeal was not successful. The Mississippi legislature then took up the issue, proposing the so-called hangman's bill, which would allow the sheriff of any county to appoint any citizen of the state as hangman. The bill was defeated. "Mississippi: Father's Right to Kill Approved by Senate."

What if the group is the would-be lynch mob gathered outside the Hernando jail? The moral views that it wanted to see inscribed in law were reprehensible and deserve unstinting rebuke, to be sure. Milling about with the would-be lynch mob in Hernando were vile racists of the worst sort. It is important to note that clarity on the racism of the lynching crowd has come with time, however. When the phenomenon of lynching initially appeared in the South it was not synonymous with racism. Ida B. Wells, who became one of the most vocal and persistent critics of lynching, initially did not see lynching as a mechanism of racism. Wells's realization about the racial injustice of lynching only came after she began concertedly investigating lynchings. There is a deeper problem here too. Unless someone (the righteous? the government? the intelligentsia?) can control morality and definitively eradicate vile values, it is possible that the citizenry of a democratic polity will adopt reprehensible beliefs. This has certainly happened with sufficient frequency in the past to make it a distinct possibility in the future. This prospect, no doubt, is one reason to study the post-Reconstruction South, to recall its injustices, and to understand how racial inequality was sustained and justified. Still, the fact that popular morality changes (and not always for the better) is a significant and intractable problem for democratic theories that link law and popular will.

I do not have a solution to the predicament posed by reprehensible popular morality and make no suggestion here as to how to address it. My more modest goal is to explore the relationship between citizens, law, and popular morality by taking account of a concrete case of malevolent popular morality, lynching in the post-Reconstruction South. How did lynching crowds conceptualize the relationship between their morality and the law? How did their normative idea of moral and representative law differ from that of civil disobedients in the civil rights movement? To address these questions, it is essential to demonstrate, first, that some lynchings were intended to express popular morality and that some lynchers, like the would-be lynching crowd in Hernando, hoped to change law through the force of their moral convictions and their numbers. Second, it is crucial to demonstrate that the civil rights movement also fashioned itself as a group of moral citizens who represented the mores of a much larger local constituency. It too relied on moral conviction and numbers. Third and finally, seeing the similarities between how lynching crowds and the civil rights movement understood the role of popular morality reveals crucial differences. These are particularly apparent around what H.L.A. Hart called power-conferring rules—that is, rules in a legal system that explain how law is identified, changed, and adjudicated. Lynch mobs understood that a morally indignant people, as a single and uniform moral force, could properly intervene in power-conferring rules.

Civil disobedients in the civil rights movement, in contrast, were reluctant to either violate or change power-conferring rules.

Vox Populi: Mass Lynch Mobs

Lynching cases and the rhetoric that surrounded them are the natural places to gain insight into the populist side of southern lynch mobs. Yet, a focus on lynching cases and what was said about them is prone to several difficulties. First, there are many cases. The latest comprehensive quantitative study of lynching documents nearly three thousand victims from 1882 to 1930.[8] What's more, these three thousand cases are varied because lynch mobs adopted a range of methods. There were four general types of lynch mobs in the South: terrorist mobs based in secret organizations (i.e., Ku Kluxers), private mobs of family or friends that sought vengeance, quasi-legal lynching mobs conducted by posses, and public lynching mobs.[9] Not too surprisingly, the variety of tactics employed by lynch mobs makes it difficult to draw broad conclusions about lynching in the South.

In addition the historical record of southern lynchings is not always trustworthy. Newspaper articles, memoirs, magazine articles, and popular accounts of lynchings lapse at times into what one scholar has provocatively referred to as a "folk pornography"—that is, a titillating story of interracial rape that was either partially or wholly untrue.[10] In such cases, a salacious and widely accepted story, typically of a black man raping a white woman, hid what really occurred. Sometimes the rape never took place;

[8] Tolnay and Beck, *Festival of Violence*, ix. Tolnay and Beck identify 2,805 victims of lynching in ten Southern states from 1992 to 1930. Of this total, approximately 300 were white men and women; 155 were the victims of a presumed black or integrated lynch mob. It is important to note that Tolnay and Beck's count of lynching victims is more conservative than most. Earlier researchers typically cite 3,000 to 4,000 victims.

[9] Terrorist and private mobs typically were secretive and involved fewer than fifty participants. Posse mobs, in contrast, were organized and authorized by local law enforcement. They killed the accused, rather than capturing him. The final type that I focus on in this chapter—public lynch mobs—operated in broad daylight, emphasized ritual, attracted large crowds, and garnered widespread local and regional attention. Brundage, *Lynching in the New South*, 17–48.

[10] Hall, *Revolt against Chivalry*, 150–51. The historical record has also been altered for less nefarious reasons. In *100 Years of Lynchings*, a documentary history that reprinted hundreds of press accounts of lynchings in the South, Ralph Ginzburg noted that he edited some documents. Some articles, he wrote, "have been drastically rewritten for the sake of clarity or conciseness. . . . In cases where two or more newspapers contained different—but not conflicting—information, the information from all sources has been synthesized into one story and attributed to the newspaper which provided most of the facts." Ginzburg, *100 Years of Lynchings*, 5–6.

sometimes the relationship was consensual. In either case, fiction passed as fact. Adding to this problem, it is not always clear *which* accounts of lynchings are true and which false. Looking at a stack of newspaper accounts, for instance, it is not obvious which articles provide accurate information and which do not.[11]

With these problems in mind, I've selected two cases where the facts are clear. In both cases a reliable and unsympathetic source provided a detailed account of what occurred shortly after the lynching.[12] Also, these two cases are representative of a particular *kind* of lynching in the South, not all lynchings. Both of the cases I examine were public mass lynchings in which mobs of more than fifty members killed with comparative ceremony and made no attempt to hide their actions or their identities. This subset of cases is particularly interesting because mass lynchings were typically what southerners thought of when they debated the merits of lynching. Moreover, they were fairly common. In Georgia, for instance, mass lynchings were the most common type.[13]

The first case occurred in Newnan, Georgia, a town about forty miles southeast of Atlanta, in July of 1899. Difficulties began when Samuel Hose, a black laborer, requested an advance in pay from Alfred Cranford, his white employer. Hose and Cranford quarreled, and Hose's request was denied. The following day while Hose was chopping wood, Cranford resumed the argument. It is unclear why the dispute escalated, though Cranford was said to have a quick temper. In the heat of the clash, weapons were drawn: Cranford drew his pistol and Hose threw the ax. Hose's aim was better. As Cranford lay dead in the yard, Hose fled into the woods seeking refuge near his mother's house. When Hose was cap-

[11] There is an additional problem. The press used "lynching" to mean different things in different periods. See Waldrep, "War of Words."

[12] In the first case, Ida B. Wells-Barnett, the well-known and intrepid critic of lynchings, hired a white private investigator to track down the details of the lynching of Sam Hose (also called Sam Holt and Samuel Wilkes) in Newnan, Georgia, in 1899. The detective traveled to Newnan to conduct interviews with witnesses, to confirm various accounts of the crime, and to look for inconsistencies and holes in the story about Hose. Wells-Barnett, "Detective's Report." Also see "Mrs. Alfred Cranford Talks." For an overview of the case and a discussion of Wells-Barnett's involvement, see Dray, *At the Hands of Persons Unknown*, 3–16. Leon Litwack also discusses the Hose case in his introduction to Allen, *Without Sanctuary*. In the second case, the federal district court in Tampa, Florida, recorded the facts of a lynching in Tampa in the 1882 circuit court case *In Re Wall* and the 1883 Supreme Court case *Ex Parte Wall*. The *Wall* case concerned the disbarment of a prominent local attorney, J. B. Wall, who allegedly participated in the lynching of Charles Owens in front of the Tampa federal district court in 1882. *Ex Parte Wall, 107 U.S. 265 (1883)*; *In Re Wall, 13 F. 814 (1882)*.

[13] Georgia public lynchings accounted for 34 percent of lynchings in the state, while in Virginia they accounted for 40 percent of the lynchings. Brundage, *Lynching in the New South*, 36.

tured and arrested a few days later, public sentiment against him was pronounced.[14] In large part this was because the local press published an incorrect account of the crime, reporting that Hose had killed Cranford in cold blood and had raped Mrs. Cranford. Local newspaper articles reveled in the graphic details of this make-believe offense. In depicting the alleged crime for its readership, an article in the *Atlanta Constitution* reported that the "wife was seized, choked, thrown upon the floor, where her clothing lay in the blood of her husband, and ravished." The article implored readers to keep in mind the picture of "Mrs. Cranford outraged in the blood of her murdered husband."[15] This erroneous account of Hose's crime was reiterated far and wide and was generally accepted as true.[16]

Indignant about the monstrosity of Hose's fabricated crimes, a mob reportedly composed of individuals "from every house in the little city" charged the jail.[17] Though the mob encountered resistance—both the sheriff and a former governor of Georgia attempted to dissuade it from lawlessness—it successfully kidnapped Hose. Rather than killing him immediately, the mob bided its time waiting for masses of spectators to arrive the following day, a Sunday, on special excursion trains from Atlanta. According to the account in the *Atlanta Constitution*, two thousand witnessed Hose's death.[18] The killing itself was brutal and ritualistic: Hose, chained to tree and stripped of his clothes, was tortured as the mob cut off his fingers and ears and plunged knives into his flesh.[19] He was eventually burned alive. If the mob felt any remorse or shame about the brutality of

[14] A former employer, J. B. Jones, turned Hose over to the authorities. Reports vary as to how many others were involved in the capture. Wells reported that Jones turned in Hose with six others, including his brother, J. L. Jones. Wells-Barnett, "The Detective's Report." Other accounts reported that the "Jones brothers" turned Hose in. "Negro Burned at a Tree."

[15] "Negro Burned at a Tree." According to Wells, a local businessman, E. D. Sharkey, was the source of the misinformation about the rape of Mrs. Cranford. Wells-Barnett, "The Detective's Report." This account is repeated in "Mob after Hose." For more on the depiction of Hose and the embellishments of the crime, see Brundage, *Lynching in the New South*, 82–85.

[16] The erroneous account of Hose's crime appeared in a number of publications outside of Atlanta and the South, including the *New York Times*, the *Boston Evening Transcript* and the Congressional Record of the House of Representatives. See *Congressional Record*, 56th Cong., 1st sess., February 1, 1900.

[17] "Negro Burned at a Tree."

[18] "Sam Holt, Murderer and Assailant, Burned at the Stake at Newnan."

[19] The methodical actions of the mob that lynched Hose can be obscured by calling it a "mob." Catherine Holland notes, "the notion of mob violence associated with lynching—with its evocation of angry, unruly, and disorganized vigilante action—tends to obscure the degree to which lynch mobs also routinely engaged in highly organized, systematic, and stylized rituals of judgment, punishment, and collective purification." Holland, *The Body Politic*, 154.

its acts, it gave no sign of it. As with other public mass lynchings, the participants were unmasked, and they killed in broad daylight before scores of witnesses. What's more, several prominent elites were involved in Hose's killing, and, like the other participants, they made no attempt to hide their identities.[20]

Hose's lynching lays bare the virulent racism of some southern whites, to be sure. Deep-seated racial hatred influenced Hose's mistreatment from his fateful quarrel with Cranford to the inaccurate description of his crimes to his ritualistic killing before a crowd of angry whites. Given the degree of racism in the South, it is perhaps not too surprising that none of Hose's killers were indicted, much less prosecuted or convicted.[21] And it is also safe to surmise that this racially prejudiced killing terrorized a good portion of the local African American community into a fearful subservience. It is unlikely that a black employee in the greater Atlanta area made any requests for a salary advance, or anything else for that matter, from white employers for some time to come.

But racism was not the only idea uniting Hose's lynch mob. In addition to being racist, the mob that lynched Hose was also a populist group that sought to articulate the moral values and principles of a sizable group of ordinary white residents in the greater Atlanta area.[22] The lynch mob's populist ambitions may have just been ambitions. Did the mob represent the moral views of all whites in the area? The sheriff and the former governor clearly disagreed with the mob, so this certainly was not the case.[23] Nor is it likely that all the spectators of Hose's lynching shared moral

[20] On elite participation in lynchings, see Brundage, *Lynching in the New South*, 38. On elite participation in the Hose killing, see Wells-Barnett, "Detective's Report."

[21] In most Southern states lynching was not a crime, but kidnapping and murder were. Still, authorities rarely prosecuted members of lynch mobs, even in cases where their identities were known. In light of the inadequate enforcement of state and local laws, civil rights activists advocated for a federal antilynching law. For proposed versions of federal antilynching legislation, see Subcommittee of the Committee on the Judiciary, *Punishment for the Crime of Lynching*; Subcommitee of the Committee on the Judiciary, *To Prevent and Punish the Crime of Lynching*. For an overview of the fight for federal antilynching legislation, see Rable, "South and the Politics of Antilynching Legislation." For more on the civil rights activists, see Hall, *Revolt against Chivalry*; and Zangrando, *NAACP Crusade against Lynching*.

[22] For an examination of how populist and republican ideas can be allied with xenophobia and racism, see "Reactionary Populism: The Politics of Class," in MacLean, *Behind the Mask of Chivalry*; and MacLean, "Leo Frank Case Reconsidered." For a historical examination of how American civic conceptions have blended liberal, republican, and ascriptive elements, see Smith, *Civic Ideals*.

[23] The 1890s were marked by class conflict among whites. The Populist Party, for instance, articulated the economic and political interests of small farmers and laborers in opposition to the dominant class of planters, merchants, and businessmen. Inverarity, "Populism and Lynching in Louisiana"; Lane, *Murder in America*, 149–56; Woodward, *Strange Career of Jim Crow*; and Woodward, *Tom Watson*.

views about his alleged crime and punishment. Critics of lynchings were sometimes spectators, and, thus, it is difficult to draw conclusions about the moral sentiments of the crowd. Even if the lynch mob and the crowd constituted a local majory—a claim that was made to legitimate lynching violence but rarely proved—it is clear that their actions did not have the moral endorsement of all whites in the area, to say nothing of the moral approval of the African American community.

What is clear, however, is that the mob and its apologists made efforts to *appear* to represent the moral views of a sizable contingent of residents.[24] The *Atlanta Constitution*, for instance, noted that Hose's crime had agitated the people to "a high pitch of nervous excitement," and to see "the determined attitude of this people and hear the expression of public sentiment [is] to be convinced that the capture of Sam Hose means death to him and probably public torture."[25] These accounts stress that the "people" was a united and homogeneous body: It felt the same emotions (nervous excitement), it shared the same mind-set (a determined attitude), and it agreed to the same action (public lynching and torture). Indeed, another article even suggested that segments of the black community in Milner, Georgia, were allied against Hose and were making "every effort to catch him."[26] To modern ears, the suggestion that portions of the black community were united against Hose seems questionable. The veracity of this report may actually be beside the point. Whether true or not, it is clear that apologists for the lynch mob wanted to depict the freedmen

[24] The importance of communal support for lynching was emphasized in one of the earliest social-science examinations of the phenomenon, Cutler's *Lynch-Law*. Cutler defines lynching as "an illegal or summary execution at the hands of a mob, or a number of persons, who have in some degree the public opinion of the community behind them." It is "not too much to say," Cutler noted, "that popular justification is the *sine qua non* of lynching" (276). More recently, Christopher Waldrep has argued that racial violence that did not have popular support during this period did not qualify as lynching. Waldrep, *Many Faces of Judge Lynch*, 85–101; Waldrep, "War of Words." On communal support for lynching, see Brundage, *Lynching in the New South*, 36–45; Hall, *Revolt against Chivalry*, 139–41; MacLean, "Leo Frank Case Reconsidered"; McGovern, *Anatomy of a Lynching*, x.

[25] "Excitement at Palmetto." Local papers also reported that residents provided posse members with horses, mules, and bugles; citizens reportedly cheered when the posse passed. "Hose Is a Will 'O the Wisp to His Determined Pursuers." For similar details on the communal aspect of Hose's lynching itself, see "Sam Holt, Murderer and Assailant, Burned at the Stake at Newnan." For photographic evidence of the popular support of lynchings, see Allen, *Without Sanctuary*.

[26] "He Cannot Escape, They Say." On the available evidence, it is difficult to tell if the black community in Milner was actually helping the white posse tracking Hose. Freedmen and -women could have merely feigned support of the posse or they could have purposefully subverted it by giving posse members false information about Hose's whereabouts. The trouble that the posse had in locating Hose suggests the possibility of misinformation. See, for instance, "Posse Went Out to Look at Him," "Sam Holt Believed to Be Near Scene of His Crime," "Sam Holt Now Believed to Have Been Located Near Cusseta, Ala."

and -women of Milner as united with whites in their odium for Hose's alleged crimes.[27]

The importance of populist moral support of Hose's lynching is apparent not only in what proponents of the lynching said but also in what the mob itself did. In particular, the lynch mob killed Hose publicly, with ceremony and ritual in front of a crowd of spectators. The mob could have easily adopted another, more efficient method of lynching Hose.[28] The individuals who found Hose could have quickly lynched him in the Georgia woods, for instance. Posse lynchings were common enough that the men pursuing Hose might very well have considered killing him rather than turning him in to the sheriff.[29] Indeed, a newspaper article raised this concern, suggesting that Hose's captors might err by "kill[ing] him on sight" instead of turning him over to the authorities.[30]

A posse lynching held certain clear advantages over a public mass lynching. It was quick, less risky, and easier to orchestrate. None of the elaborate preparations involved in getting the crowds to Newnan and none of the decisions about how to organize and coordinate Hose's torture and killing would be necessary. Moreover, a posse lynching required a comparatively small group. A hurdle for any form of collective action is getting the parties to concur on an appropriate course of action and to cooperatively carry it out. And in this respect a posse lynching was considerably easier to accomplish than a public lynching because it involved fewer participants. Despite the advantages of a posse lynching, the mob that killed Hose adopted a more populist, demonstrative, and ritualistic method of moral condemnation.

Though more difficult to accomplish, public mass lynchings also emphasized the discord between the popular morality of the lynch mob and the law. This discord was most clear in the common confrontations between the mob and the legal authorities over possession of the alleged criminal. In Hose's case, the sheriff reportedly tried to resist the mob—a critic of the lynching called his efforts "manly" in the *New York Times*—but to no avail.[31] The mob also encountered the former governor of Geor-

[27] The tendency of white southerners to seek approval from freedmen and -women for a lynching was not as unusual as it might first appear. Southern newspapers tended to note if the victim had died at the hands of an interracial mob because this had more legitimacy. Newspapers also took care to mention by name freedmen and -women who had assisted posses or lynch mobs. Moreover, southern whites also solicited the freedmen and -women for their support of specific lynchings. See Raper, *Tragedy of Lynching*, 21. On black responses to lynching, see Ayers, *Promise of the New South*, 156–59; Beck and Tolnay, "When Race Didn't Matter"; Brundage, *Lynching in the New South*, 45–47; Shapiro, *White Violence and Black Response*.

[28] On the historical contingency of lynchings and prevented lynchings, see Griffin, Clark, and Sandberg, "Narrative and Event."

[29] Brundage, *Lynching in the New South*, 33–36.

[30] "Hose Is a Will 'O the Wisp to His Determined Pursuers."

[31] "Clerical Editor's Opinion."

gia, W. Y. Atkinson, who urged it to let the authorities proceed and argued that the law would act "quickly and effectually." Atkinson then threatened the mob with the law: "Some of you are known to me and when this affair is finally settled, you may depend upon it that I will testify against you."[32] Neither tactic worked.[33]

Contact between the mob and the authorities was a common element of lynching in the South. Of the 254 lynchings that occurred from 1921 to 1929, approximately 56 percent involved an abduction of the prisoner from the jail or in transit to the jail.[34] The figures for *public* lynchings were even higher in some states: In Georgia public lynch mobs took 72 percent of their victims from legal authorities, while in Virginia, *all* victims of public lynchings were taken from the hands of the law.[35]

These encounters between public lynch mobs and the authorities made the popular moral objections to law enforcement palpable. The Newnan sheriff did not record his experience in facing down the mob, but other officers—even those who were sympathetic to lynch mobs—were more forthcoming. In these accounts, a fairly standard story is told: A lone officer or deputy faced a sizable crowd demanding the keys to the jail and possession of the prisoner. The size of the crowd and its makeup mattered to sheriffs, all the more so to sheriffs who were elected. As one officer put it, "I went into that cellblock with every intention of fulfilling my oath and protecting that man but when the mob opened the door, the first half-a-dozen men standing there were leading citizens—businessmen, leaders of their churches and community—I just couldn't do it."[36]

While this officer was cowed by the presence of elites, others were more concerned with the size of the crowd. Greater numbers of participants meant greater electoral security if the officer complied. One local sheriff did nothing to prevent a lynching, an observer noted, because "he looked the mob over and saw back of them voters, and he saw back of that dying

[32] "Negro Burned at a Tree." Also see Ginzburg, *100 Years of Lynchings*, 13–14; "Sam Holt, Murderer and Assailant, Burned at the Stake at Newnan."

[33] In some cases law-enforcement officials did resist lynch mobs. The 1930 lynching of Allan Green in Walhalla, South Carolina, for instance, began with a confrontation between the armed sheriff protecting Green and a crowd of over one hundred vigilantes. After an exchange of words, one of the vigilantes struck the sheriff with a sharp blow to the head, while others obtained the keys to the cell and seized Green. In another lynching in the same year in Sherman, Texas, the efforts of the Texas Rangers and the local militia to thwart the lynching of George Hughes led to an open battle with the vigilantes: The courthouse was burned and the militia was kept at bay with a barrage of bricks, bottles, and wood. Raper, *Tragedy of Lynching*, 263–85 and 317–55. Also see Griffin, Clark, and Sandberg, "Narrative and Event."

[34] In 26.8 percent of cases, the prisoner was taken from the jail, while in 29.1 percent of cases the prisoner was abducted in transit. Raper, *Tragedy of Lynching*, 31–32.

[35] Brundage, *Lynching in the New South*, 39.

[36] Hall, *Revolt against Chivalry*, 140. Also see Chadbourn, *Lynching and the Law*, 58–67.

Negro nothing . . . Back of that mob was his bread and his butter and the shoes and clothes and schooling for his children, and back of that Negro nothing."[37] Though a lynching clearly wasn't an election, it could be a proxy for one, with a mob of voters implicitly threatening to withdraw future support from a sheriff who did not comply. It is perhaps not surprising that some sheriffs were explicit, even vehement, in their support of lynch mobs.[38]

A second case, the lynching of Charles D. Owens in Tampa, Florida, in 1882, is useful because it reveals populism detached from racism and illuminates an honor critique of the law. On March 5, Owens, a white itinerant, broke into the home of one of Tampa's leading businessmen, pocketed several items, and attempted to rape Ada McCarty, the businessman's twenty-six-year-old sister.[39] Owens was discovered and scared off, and in his hasty departure, he left a sheath knife and scabbard that were used to identify him. The following morning the sheriff pursued Owens and quickly apprehended him. By one in the afternoon, Owens was in jail awaiting trial.

A crowd of one hundred to two hundred quickly gathered outside of Owens's cell and called for a lynching. Surprising the sheriff at his home, the mob obtained keys to the jail, and, with the means to obtain Owens in its grasp, it considered whether he should be killed. A vote was taken. All were in favor of lynching, with the exception of the sheriff and the mayor.[40] Their objections held little sway. As one newspaper account put it, the sheriff "was as helpless as an infant in the presence of so large and determined [a] group of men led on by some [of] our most prominent citizens."[41] Buoyed by its united sense of purpose, the mob marched to the jail, hung Owens, and left his body hanging in front of the local courthouse until sunset.

[37] Hall, *Revolt against Chivalry*, 225.

[38] Asked about his failure to protect George Grant from vigilantes in Darien, Georgia, for instance, the local sheriff replied, "I don't know who killed the damn nigger and I don't care! I'm glad he's dead! Law and order! What's law and order when Mr. Nigger can kill a good white man like Freeman and try to kill a half dozen more, and then keep him in jail and give him a trial—and cost the county a whole pile of money? I'm glad he's dead; I'd liked to have killed him myself, damn nigger!" Another sheriff asked, "Do you think I'm going to risk my life protecting a nigger?" Raper, *Tragedy of Lynching*, 208, 213.

[39] Owens is referred to by name in newspaper accounts (in some press clippings he is called "Owen"). In *Ex Parte Wall*, he is referred to as "John" or "one John."

[40] The witness whose testimony is recorded in *Ex Parte Wall*, Peter A. Williams, does not mention that a vote was taken. Williams's account does confirm that the sheriff and mayor protested the lynching.

[41] "A Man Hanged in Tampa." *Ex Parte Wall* confirmed that elites were involved in Owens's lynching. The circuit court relied on the witness testimony of the U.S. marshal for the district (an unusual move to be sure); because of "the influential position of some of those engaged in the hanging, and the sympathy of others with the lynching, it was not advisable to attempt to compel any resident of said city of Tampa who was found to have personal knowledge of the matter, to testify." *Ex Parte Wall*, 270.

Owens's lynching is particularly helpful in exposing the populist values and ideas inherent in a public lynching because racism was not a factor in this case. Owens was white, as was the mob that lynched him. Same-race lynchings were not common in the South, but they were not as rare as one might first suppose. Over 10 percent of those lynched in the post-Reconstruction South were white.[42] In general, these white victims were not killed because they violated racial norms or because they were so-called nigger lovers. Rather, as the lynching of Owens suggests, white-on-white lynchings were prompted by some of the same fears and concerns as interracial lynchings: an anxiety about familial honor and protecting white feminine virtue, communal outrage over a particularly heinous crime, a loss of faith in the courts, and a deep suspicion of outsiders.[43] Further complicating the racial dimension of southern lynchings, almost 6 percent of lynching victims in the South were killed by a black or interracial mob. The victims of black or interracial mobs were overwhelmingly black. These were black-on-black lynchings, in other words.[44] And, as with white-on-white lynchings, the historical record does not suggest that racial norms or racism were particularly pronounced factors in black-on-black lynchings.[45]

In the absence of racist justifications, the southern lynch mob's populist view of the law is more apparent. Like their vigilante counterparts on the western frontier, southern lynch mobs justified their actions by attacking the local criminal-justice system and by articulating a notion of law that was rooted more firmly in the values and principles of the community.

[42] Three hundred (10.69%) of the total 2,805 lynching victims in ten Southern states from 1882 to 1930 were white men or women. Same-race lynchings are clustered in the 1880s and 1890s and decline more rapidly than interracial lynchings in the twentieth-century. In the 1880s and 1890s, for instance, two out of every ten lynching victims were killed by a mob that, in terms of race, looked like them. Tolnay and Beck, *Festival of Violence*, ix, 149.

[43] See Brundage, *Lynching in the New South*, 86–102. Also see Beck and Tolnay, "When Race Didn't Matter," 132–54. White-on-white mobs tended to lynch whites that were viewed as outsiders and deviants. Owens's lynching suggests this xenophobic tendency—Owens was both an itinerant and a recent immigrant from England—and it is suggested by other well-known white-on-white lynchings. Leo Frank, who was lynched in 1915 for raping and killing a thirteen-year-old factory worker, was a "Yankee Jew," as one observer put it. MacLean, "Gender, Sexuality, and the Politics of Lynching"; MacLean, "Leo Frank Case Reconsidered," 158. In another well-known case, the eleven whites lynched in New Orleans in 1891 after being acquitted of the murder of the police chief, were Sicilians. The ethnic identity of the victims played a clear role in their lynching: The victims were believed to be part of a Mafioso gang. Kendall, "Who Killa De Chief?"; Pfeifer, *Rough Justice*, 82–83.

[44] Only four victims of black or interracial lynch mobs were white. Tolnay and Beck, *Festival of Violence*, 269.

[45] "Murder and Lynching in Concordia Parish," "Negro Murderer Slain by Indignant Negroes," "Fiendish Negro Lynched in Bossier," "Lynching of a Ravisher-Murderer in Bienville." Also see Beck and Tolnay, "When Race Didn't Matter," and Brundage, *Lynching in the New South*, 86–102.

The lynch mob's critique of the law took two general forms, one focused on procedural inefficiencies and the other on a code of honor.

The southern lynch mobs' procedural critique of law was similar to that of frontier vigilantes. As on the frontier, southern lynch mobs complained that the law was too slow, was riddled with bureaucratic inefficiencies, and was too solicitous of the rights of criminals.[46] The law hemmed and hawed when it should have been decisive. Rather than paying attention to the community's need to see swift and certain punishment, it coddled offenders. And failing to conform to popular normative expectations about punishment and justice, the law lacked popular legitimacy. It ceased to represent the will of the people. Consider, for instance, a note pinned to the collar of a victim granted a stay of execution by the Supreme Court: "Chief Harlan—Here is your negro. Thanks for your kind consideration to him. You will find him at the morgue. THE COMMITTEE."[47] As the mob saw it, the Court, vacillating on technical criteria, would not act. The mob, on the other hand, punished with alacrity, ferocity, and impunity. Another member of a lynch mob responded similarly to a lawyer's plea to let the law take its course. "That's a lawyer talkin' now! We know that tune. The lawyers has things their own way in a courthouse."[48]

This indictment of legal dilly-dallying was pervasive enough—and, more to the point, taken seriously enough—that a range of lawyers and jurists, including Supreme Court Justice David Brewer and legal reformer Roscoe Pound, examined the roots of popular dissatisfaction with the law and considered how the American legal system should be transformed in response.[49] It is crucial to note, however, that the claim that lynch mobs had to act, especially against freedmen and -women, because the law failed to, has not been borne out by current research. Recent statistical

[46] There is little evidence that the procedural critique was valid. Southern courts were not particularly inefficient nor did they cosset black defendants. Southern legal officials executed approximately 2,500 individuals between 1882 and 1930. Almost 2,000 of those executed were black. Tolnay and Beck, *Festival of Violence*, 100. The case of black or interracial lynch mobs, which accounted for almost 6 percent of lynchings in the South, was arguably different. In particular, the arguments of black participants in lynchings that the law was effectively absent for them had more validity. The law *was* often ineffective and corrupt for African Americans in the post-Reconstruction South.

[47] "Supreme Court Openly Defied in Chattanooga." Harlan was an associate justice, not chief justice.

[48] Williamson, *Crucible of Race*, 186.

[49] Southern lawyers and judges, for instance, considered how to mitigate the appeal of lynching by reforming the criminal justice system to bring about a swifter and surer form of punishment. Bonaparte, "Lynch Law and Its Remedy"; Brewer, "Some Follies in Our Criminal Procedure"; Clark, "True Remedy for Lynch Law"; Lewis et al., "Is Lynch Law Due to Defects in the Criminal Law, or Its Administration?" 164–97. Supreme Court Justice David Brewer and legal scholar Roscoe Pound took a similar approach, arguing for various procedural reforms that addressed an overly lax right of appeal, archaic legal procedures, and

analysis has found that "lynch mobs appear to be impressively insensitive to the vigor with which the state imposed the death penalty on blacks."[50] The problem of political efficacy, at least as to the death penalty on blacks, was more imagined than real.

In addition to this procedural critique of the law, southern lynch mobs advanced a second line of legal attack that focused on the inadequacy of the law to address violations of honor. There were some grave offenses to honor, lynch mobs asserted, that could never be adequately addressed by the formal legal procedures of the law but rather required popular redress.[51] Offenses like Owens's, for instance, that violated the honor of a white woman and the sanctity of the home demanded a terrifying punishment that only the people rising up in their collectivity could adequately deliver. Protecting loved ones and the home were duties "above and beyond all law," according to one proponent, and the people were "determined to so deal with such outrages, that every wretch who is capable of committing them shall know that retribution swift and terrible, hangs like the sword of Damocles, suspended over his head by a single hair."[52] Violations of honor were, in other words, breaches of deeper and more primal social values, and the demands of retribution and deterrence necessitated an equally primal form of punishment.[53]

The honor critique of law made by Owens's lynch mob and others was more cutting than the procedural critique. The honor argument focused on the inherent limitations of the law as opposed to procedural problems in its

---

the procedural waste encompassed by a federal system. Brewer, "Right of Appeal"; Pound, "Causes of Popular Dissatisfaction with the Administration of Justice," 337–53. For these legal elites, the procedural critique of the lynch mob had merit. For more on southern critiques of the law and the connections between lynching and the legal system, see Bodenhamer and Ely, *Ambivalent Legacy*, 14–23.

[50] Tolnay and Beck, *Festival of Violence*, 112.

[51] Honor in the South was also used to justify other extralegal forms of punishment and violence, such as charivari, a Southern practice in which a mob serenaded an unconventional bride and groom by making a tremendous ruckus on their wedding night, and dueling. As with lynching, charivari and dueling were understood to address violations to honor that could not be properly addressed through ordinary legal channels. On law and honor in the antebellum South, see Ayers, *Vengeance and Justice*; Sydnor, "Southerner and the Laws"; Wyatt-Brown, *Southern Honor*. For more on honor in the Owens case, see Ingalls, "Lynching and Establishment Violence in Tampa"; Ingalls, *Urban Vigilantes in the New South*, 5–10.

[52] "Judge Locke V. General Wall." The editorial goes on to argue that a popular punishment like lynching was especially effective at delivering retribution and encouraging deterrence to an offense of honor.

[53] An honor critique more naturally fit the facts of Owens's case than a procedural critique. It would have been difficult for the mob to assert that the plodding character of the law and courts would effectively deny justice. The sheriff had apprehended Owens with great alacrity and it is likely that the local courts would have proceeded quickly too. Florida's sixth judicial circuit court was scarcely overburdened. The grand jury handed down one criminal indictment in all of 1881. Ingalls, *Urban Vigilantes in the New South*, 3–4.

execution. An early explanation of an honor critique in 1835, for instance, emphasized that lynchings could address a wider scope of harms. To

> proceed against [the offender]. . . would have been mere mockery, inasmuch as, not having the had the opportunity of consummating his design, no adequate punishment could have been inflicted on him. Consequently it was determined to take him to the woods and Lynch [*sic*] him—which is a mode of punishment provided for such as become obnoxious in a manner that the law cannot reach.[54]

To put it differently, an honor critique did not suggest any improvements or reforms of the law; there was nothing to fix in the legal system. Instead, an honor critique suggested that lynching would end only when crimes to honor ended. The onus of ending lynching rested primarily with the African American community. According to this argument, the virtuous members of the black community needed to more effectively educate and control the more deviant members.[55] Moreover, this view understood that institutionalized law was deficient in something that public lynch mobs naturally possessed—that is, the unambiguous wrath of the people. Apologists for the lynching of Leo Frank argued, for instance, that the commutation of his sentence "rob[bed] the law of part of its terror" and that the lynching preserved fear of the law.[56] Thus, according to an honor critique, popular punishments like lynchings could logically coexist with sheriffs, jails, judges, and executioners as an augmentation of these formal legal institutions.[57] Here again, lynch mobs stressed the populist aspect of their violence, though not as a corrective to law's failures but as a legitimate addition to the law. Accounts of Owens's lynching stressed, for instance, that the mob represented the "public sentiment of [the] county" and that its actions were called the "*ultima ratio populi*," the ultimate sanction of the people.[58] Defenses of the mob's action underscored that it was not composed of an uninformed rabble overtaken by passion and excitement. The "honorable and law abiding people" of the mob that lynched Owens exercised "mature deliberation." And these defenses, like the mob itself, claimed to represent "*vox populi*."[59] The mob could express what the law could not: the popular and primal outrage of the people.

[54] Hofstadter and Wallace, *American Violence*, 451.

[55] See, for instance, "Governor Blames the Negroes."

[56] MacLean, "Leo Frank Case Reconsidered," 944.

[57] The lines between an honor critique and a procedural critique are often blurred in contemporary accounts. A focus on honor did not necessarily preclude complaints about the protracted nature of legal proceedings. In Owens' case, for instance, the *Jacksonville Union* (reprinted in the *Tampa Sunland Tribune*) observed that there are "some crimes [so] dastardly and revolting as to fatigue the public indignation," and concluded "it is hardly surprising that in this instance the people of Tampa felt that the law's delay would be an unmerited luxury to the felon." "Judge Locke V. General Wall."

[58] Quoted in Ingalls, *Urban Vigilantes in the New South*, 12.

[59] "Judge Locke V. General Wall."

In either case, a procedural or honor critique tended to place ultimate power over the law in the hands of the people. Popular sentiment was what gave the law its power and meaning; it was the ultimate source and impetus for the law. As one leader of a lynching put it, "When the law is powerless, the rights delegated by the people are relegated back to the people, and they are justified in doing that which the courts have failed to do." A compatriot was even more blunt: "The law had proven a farce and a mockery. It now reverts to us to take upon ourselves the right of self-preservation."[60] Since the government was unable to protect citizens from (allegedly) violent offenders, it was up to the people.

This populist conception of the origins of law was linked to a confidence in the moral character of the lynch mob. Lynch mobs and their apologists were sure that they "represented popular local feeling" and had the support of "both men and women of highest Christian character, not only in the South, but in every part of the country where lynching has been resorted to."[61] Both a belief in the mob's radical political sovereignty and a certainty of its moral authority justified lynchings. So long as both existed, one commentator noted, it would be difficult to convince lynch mobs to rely on the courts.

> We are probably far distant from the day when the people directly affected by the shock of an outrageous crime . . . will accept the cold truth that vengeance, in a legal sense, belongs exclusively and of right to the slow and pottering courts. The viper's sting automatically enforces the contact of the grinding heel, the crushing of the flattened head; even the bite of a musquito [*sic*] moves the giant's hand to the stroke of vengeance.[62]

There was, in this author's view, something irrepressible about the mob's desire to exact revenge and to make its moral condemnation of the crime and the criminal known. Like the giant's hand slapping at the sting of a bug, the people would take vengeance themselves.

Vox Populi (Part 2): The Civil Rights Movement

With a better understanding of the populist motivations behind public mass lynchings, it is now possible to examine the populist predispositions of the civil rights movement. Just as the racism of southern lynch mobs can eclipse the populist aspect of their violence, the higher-law morality of the civil rights movement can also effectively obscure the extent to which it gained legitimacy because of the support of ordinary citizens.

[60] Kendall, "Who Killa De Chief?" 520.
[61] Thomas, "Court of Judge Lynch."
[62] Ibid., 261.

Like lynch mobs, the civil disobedients that protested in Albany, Birmingham, Selma, and elsewhere were part of a well-organized and committed mass movement whose members were willing to break the law publicly and collectively.

As the historical record of the civil rights movement's organizing efforts makes abundantly clear, the number of civil disobedients and protesters at marches, rallies, sit-ins, kneel-ins, and wade-ins was a central concern.[63] Like lynch mobs, civil disobedients were clearly not a national or even a local majority. Still, the movement was most effective when it became a sizable local group. One or two disobedients were not enough, even if they were particularly dedicated and well-meaning. The power of civil disobedience as a form of resistance was predicated in part on the fact that these were public spectacles in which a significant number of citizens defied the law.[64]

The movement's commitment to raising sizable crowds of committed disobedients was partly strategic. It needed massive numbers of demonstrators who were willing to be incarcerated for a number of days in order to flood the jails and significantly impede the criminal-justice system of a targeted city. After much difficulty, this strategy eventually worked. In Birmingham, for instance, authorities were forced to house-arrest civil disobedients in a county detention home and the state fairgrounds. The strain on Birmingham's facilities was clear. And the movement's quick-witted leadership did not hesitate to use the overcrowding as yet another example of the inequitable treatment of African Americans. As photographs of the crowded conditions were printed in newspapers, King and others complained of "1,200 boys and girls, men and women languish[ing] in filthy jails."[65]

The movement leadership was also looking for a particular kind of crowd, one composed of disciplined, solid-looking citizens. Massive crowds of decent, upstanding disobedients made for better photographs and bet-

[63] The elaborate organizing plan that Wyatt Tee Walker presented to the Southern Christian Leadership Conference for the Birmingham campaign, for instance, emphasized the importance of numerous and well-organized protesters. Walker estimated that the movement needed to put upward of one thousand people in jail at one time. Even assuming that every protestor would be arrested—an assumption that no doubt exaggerates the efficiency of the Birmingham police—it is clear that the movement was committed to drawing out large crowds of disobedients. Branch, *Parting the Waters*, 689–93. It is estimated that 70,000 individuals participated in civil disobedience demonstrations and that 4,000 were arrested. Klarman, *From Jim Crow to Civil Rights*, 373.

[64] The press at times accidentally inflated the number of participants at civil rights events. Reporters counted *all* African Americans in attendance, despite the fact that some of those present were merely curious spectators. The movement leadership did not attempt to correct these press reports. Indeed, Wyatt Walker, the organizational mastermind of the Birmingham campaign, used the tendency to inflate the crowd to his advantage. He purposely delayed events in order to attract the maximum number of spectators. Branch, *Parting the Waters*, 730.

[65] "Birmingham Talks Pushed."

ter publicity. One of the most famous photographs of the period features just such a solid citizen. In it, a well-dressed and clean-cut young black man, Walter Gadsden, is held by a police officer while a police dog lunges at his midsection. Standing at the ready, another German shepherd, held back by a second officer, is prepared to attack. In the background, a crowd of well-turned-out African American men and women turn to look. A black man in a suit and hat turns on his heel to get a better look, and an older black woman dressed in a patterned skirt and a pressed white top stares. This photograph, which made President Kennedy "sick," caught the public's attention because the subject was so clearly an upstanding young man.[66] Public lynch mobs used similar tactics. Photographs of public lynchings often emphasized the size of the mob as well as its steady and determined nature. Many of these photographs, which were sometimes distributed as postcards in a grassroots effort at publicity, show a sea of seemingly decent, stone-faced whites facing the camera while the body of the victim dangles from a tree or post above. Aside from the body, these photographs could be mistaken for membership pictures of any local organization or club of the day.[67]

Public lynch mobs also strategically used their size to stymie law enforcement. They did not hope to flood the jails, however; they used their numbers to avoid it. Their hope was that with so many participants complicit in the crime, no one individual would be held responsible. Local authorities typically agreed and chose not to arrest participants in lynchings even when their guilt was not in dispute. As Mississippi governor Theodore Bilbo brusquely put it after a series of brutal lynchings in 1928, "I have neither the time nor the money to investigate 2,000 people."[68]

In addition to these strategic concerns, a sizable crowd of disciplined disobedients lent moral validity to the civil rights movement. Greater numbers suggested that the movement was not a flighty or fly-by-night operation but rather that it had a serious moral message that resonated with a considerable and dedicated constituency.[69] On this point, the movement

[66] Klarman, *From Jim Crow to Civil Rights*, 434. As the clothes and demeanor of the subject of this famous photograph suggested, Walter Gadsden was an upstanding young man from a prosperous family. Gadsden was not, as it turned out, a stalwart supporter of the civil rights movement. His encounter with the police dog convinced him that he had been "mixing with a bad crowd," and he vowed to change his behavior. Branch, *Parting the Waters*, 760–61. On the significance of this photograph, see Bosmajian and Bosmajian, *Rhetoric of the Civil-Rights Movement*, 14–15; Wexler, *Civil Rights Movement*, 170–76.

[67] Allen, *Without Sanctuary*.

[68] "Shame to Mississippi."

[69] The opposite was true as well. When the movement looked thinly constituted and unorganized, it received negative press. Critical newspaper accounts dogged the movement for much of the Birmingham campaign, for instance, because the movement looked spontaneous and unorganized. Moreover, until the involvement of schoolchildren in Birmingham, the number of protesters was small. Branch, *Parting the Waters*, 708–711, 756–802.

disagreed with Thoreau, who, though he was certainly a great inspiration to civil disobedients, took a different position on the question of numbers.[70] In Thoreau's view the disobedience of a single individual was morally significant. "It is not so important that many should be as good as you," he noted, "as that there should be some absolute goodness somewhere, for that will leaven the whole lump." For Thoreau, resistance to government could be undertaken alone—as Thoreau's solitary stint in the Concord jail suggested—because a single good individual could change the whole. As Thoreau saw it, a corrupt government did not stand much of a chance. The government "has not the vitality and force of a single living man; for a single man can bend it to his will."[71]

For Thoreau, collective action, organization, and mobilization—in short, the validation of others—were not necessary. Indeed, he suggested that courting the respect or agreement of others was beside the point. Thoreau criticized the abolitionists, for instance, for attempting to convince the majority in Massachusetts of the moral validity of their position. "I think it is enough that they have God on their side," he wrote. "Any man more right than his neighbors," he concluded "constitutes a majority of one already."[72] A higher-law critique of positive law did not depend on popular support to be authoritative. What Thoreau stressed instead of popular validation and collective action was the accuracy of an individual's notion of higher law. The point was to be *right*, not to have popular backing. Thus, a higher-law invalidation of law can be legitimate regardless of whether one person believes it to be true or 5 million do. There is, Thoreau asserted, "little virtue in the action of masses of men."[73]

[70] On Thoreau's influence on the civil rights movement, see Branch, *Parting the Waters*, 144, 262, 279; Laue, *Direct Action and Desegregation*, 60–61; Levy, *Documentary History of the Modern Civil Rights Movement*, 82–83; Wexler, *Civil Rights Movement*, 71.

[71] Thoreau, *Higher Law*, 69, 61. Yet, it is important to note that, as Thoreau saw it, most individuals did not see the point in resisting government. The "mass of men serve the State" and have "no free exercise whatever of the judgment or of the moral sense; but they put themselves on a level with wood and earth and stones." They "command no more respect than men of straw, or a lump of dirt. They have the same sort of worth only as horses and dogs" (66).

[72] Ibid., 74. Thoreau's individualism is also apparent in his discussion of the virtue of democracy and the social-contract tradition. Both, as he sees it, provide a deeper respect for the individual. A just government

> must have the sanction and the consent of the governed. It can have no pure right over my person and property but what I concede to it. The progress from an absolute to a limited monarchy, from a limited monarchy to a democracy, is a progress toward a true respect for the individual. . . . There will never be a really free and enlightened State, until the State comes to recognize the individual as a higher and independent power, from which all its own power and authority are derived, and treats him accordingly. (89)

[73] Ibid., 70. Elsewhere in "Resistance to Civil Goverment," Thoreau underscored that the masses acting through the government were his adversary: "I was not born to be forced. I

Indeed, according to Thoreau, the lone individual protesting the law was not only a legitimate force for change, but also a very effective one. A single individual acting alone was, in his view, capable of initiating significant political change. "I know this well . . . if *one* HONEST man, in this State of Massachusetts, *ceasing to hold slaves*, were actually to withdraw from this co-partnership, and be locked up in the county jail therefore, it would be the abolition of slavery in America."[74] It is not clear from Thoreau's account, how this change would occur (or, more to the point, why it had not occurred when Thoreau was locked up in the Concord jail).[75] No doubt much of what Thoreau said on this score was hyperbole. Still, he clearly believed in the political efficacy of the individual.

In keeping with Thoreau's vision, some activists in the civil rights era did take an individualistic approach. One such heir of Thoreau's was William Moore, a white postman from Baltimore who walked from Chattanooga to Mississippi wearing signboards proclaiming "END SEGREGATION IN AMERICA" and "EQUAL RIGHTS FOR ALL MEN."[76] Moore's autonomous act of protest did not go well. In the midst of his trek, he was shot twice in the head at close range and killed. In addition, Moore's sanity was questioned when reporters discovered that he had been confined for more than a year to a mental hospital. As a result, Moore looked more like an unbalanced individual than a dedicated activist driven by deeply felt moral beliefs.

Moore's example is illuminating because it suggests that, in the spirit of Thoreau's individualism, the movement might have adopted a different strategy of resistance altogether. It might have simply issued a moral call

will breathe after my own fashion. Let us see who is the strongest. What force has a multitude? They only can force me who obey a higher law than I. They force me to become like themselves. I do not hear of *men* being *forced* to live this way or that by masses of men" (Ibid., 80–81, emphasis original).

[74] Ibid., 75. Thoreau also emphasized the effectiveness of *individual* action for both the ordinary citizen and the government official. "When the subject has refused allegiance, and the officer has resigned his office, then the revolution is accomplished" (77).

[75] Elsewhere Thoreau suggests that true withdrawal from the social contract may be more difficult than disobeying the law and spending time behind bars. As he puts it, "If I had known how to name them, I should then have signed off in detail from all the societies which I never signed on to; but I did not know where to find such a complete list" (ibid., 79).

[76] Moore did not choose to act alone. He had petitioned the Congress for Racial Equality for support but his request was refused. Branch, *Parting the Waters*, 747–51. James Meredith's plan to march 220 miles from Memphis, Tennessee, to Jackson, Mississippi, in 1966 is another example of an individual of conscience protesting more in the spirit of Thoreau. Meredith's solo "March against Fear" was intended to inspire his fellow African Americans to stand up to white authority and to encourage them to register to vote. He was shot (but not killed) thirty miles into his march. See Meredith's "Statement" for his tendency to speak of the struggle for integration in individual terms, in Levy, *Documentary History of the Modern Civil Rights Movement*, 49.

to arms and urged sympathizers to take action in whatever way they individually deemed appropriate. One can imagine that resistance and disobedience would be more spontaneous, creative, and heterogeneous as individuals chose to express their discontent in various ways. Yet the movement did not adopt a less structured and less collectivist approach to disobedience and dissent. And in light of cases like Moore's, the movement's choice to organize collectively—to hold a seemingly innumerable number of community meetings, to develop a concerted plan of action, to actively recruit volunteers to disobey the law in a specific, disciplined way, and so on—seems significant.[77]

The movement's departure from Thoreau's individualism, which is fairly clear in terms of tactics, also suggests a different understanding of a higher-law critique. While Thoreau's vision of higher law is centered on the individual, the movement's notion of higher law was more collectivist and populist. Consider, for instance, the distinct ways that each comes to know higher law and to apprehend a conflict between higher and positive law. For Thoreau, the individual of conscience needs to ask herself basically one question: Do I understand the dictates of higher law correctly? Or, alternatively, is God on my side? If the answer to this question is yes, then disobedience to the offending positive laws is justified.

The movement's theoretical understanding of how to apprehend higher law extended beyond the boundaries of the individual, however. The questions that it asked were: Do we, as a group, have a similar understanding of the dictates of higher law? And, does this shared understanding of higher law *and* our commitment to one another warrant disobedience to an unjust law? The decision to act as a group, not as individuals, put additional restrictions on their conception of higher law: It had to be shared among disobedients—at least loosely so—and it had to inspire a commitment to act together as a group.[78] The movement's method of understanding higher law, to put the point differently, was horizontal, while Thoreau's approach was vertical. By this, I mean that the movement developed and articulated its vision of higher law through members who were comparatively equal to one another. Its higher-law commitments were

[77] For arguments that stress the collective and political nature of the civil rights movement, see Bosmajian and Bosmajian, *Rhetoric of the Civil-Rights Movement*, 7–13; Branch, *Parting the Waters*, 689–802; Carson, *Movement*, ix-xi; Klarman, *From Jim Crow to Civil Rights*, 377–84; Lakey, *Strategy for a Living Revolution*, 160–66; Laue, *Direct Action and Desegregation*, 113–32; Tracy, *Direct Action*.

[78] This was an *ideal* the civil rights movement often fell short of attaining. Civil disobedients did not always have a shared sense of moral purpose and, as with all groups, individuals joined for a variety of reasons. At some points too their resolve to act together broke. The movement's consistent efforts to correct for these shortcomings through more training, more meetings, and more outreach suggests that it did strive for a degree of agreement about why and how to disobey.

shared across a group of citizens who were similarly situated.[79] Thoreau's individual disobedient, on the other hand, communed with God, a higher-law document like the Bible or Constitution, or some other higher power that transcended the individual.[80] King and other leaders of the movement did, of course, make frequent references to Christian ethics, theology, and God's commands, and there is little doubt that many disobedients in the movement were motivated by a belief in a higher power. They, too, had a vertical understanding of higher law. Still, if this vertical conception of higher law had been sufficient, then one would expect King to have protested, like Moore and Thoreau, by himself. Instead, he sought to develop a shared understanding of higher-law commands and to find common ground among a sizable group of citizens.

The movement's collectivist and populist approach to disobedience resulted in showdowns with the police that, at least structurally, were similar to those encountered by public lynch mobs. And as with lynch mobs, the collective will of the civil disobedients occasionally triumphed over legal authorities. Consider, for instance, an encounter with the local authorities that King and others in the movement identified as a (if not the) crucial turning point in the Birmingham campaign.[81] King recalled the march to Julius Ellsberry Park and the subsequent face-off with the authorities as "one of the most fantastic events in the Birmingham story."[82] Among the rank and file of the movement, the march to Ellsberry Park was called a miracle, which was akin to the parting of the Red Sea.[83]

[79] The civil rights movement also relied on and often presented its vision of higher law in vertical terms, that is, it justified its view of higher law by appealing to the Bible or to God's commands. And there were vertical relationships within the movement between the leadership and the membership. It was not an entirely egalitarian enterprise, in other words, and God was clearly an important influence. My point is simply that the relationships within the movement were more egalitarian and horizontal than the relationship between an individual and God.

[80] Addressing the issue of how one apprehends higher law, Thoreau wrote, "They who know of no purer sources of truth, who have traced up its stream no higher, stand, and wisely stand, by the Bible and the Constitution, and drink at it there with reverence and humility; but they who behold where it comes trickling into the lake or that pool, gird up their loins once more, and continue their pilgrimage toward its fountain-head." Thoreau, *Higher Law*, 88.

[81] King's arrest and his *Letter from Birmingham Jail* might also seem to be a significant turning point in the Birmingham campaign. At the time, however, the influence of King's arrest and the *Letter* were not immediately felt. The movement continued to receive negative press after King's arrest, and the *Letter* was not widely known. The black press and national media did not mention it until more than a month after it was written. In June 24, 1963, more than two months after it was composed, the *Letter* was published in the *New Leader*. Levy, *Documentary History of the Modern Civil Rights Movement*, 109. It is important to note that the eventual success of the movement in Birmingham saved the *Letter* from obscurity, not the other way around. Branch, *Parting the Waters*, 744.

[82] King, *Why We Can't Wait*, 100–101.

[83] Branch, *Parting the Waters*, 766–68.

The march to Ellsberry Park did not look like a miracle from the start. Indeed, it began as a typical demonstration. After a two-hour prayer meeting at the Sixteenth Street Baptist Church, approximately two thousand demonstrators poured onto the street with the goal of marching to the city jail to show support for the more than a thousand disobedients who had been arrested over the previous few days.[84] Wearing their Sunday best, the crowd marched down Sixth Avenue toward the jail, singing and laughing. About a block short of their destination at the barrier between the "colored" and white sections of town, the commissioner of public safety, Eugene "Bull" Connor, stood before a barricade of pump engines and a phalanx of officers ready to turn their fire hoses on the crowd.[85] Connor ordered the demonstrators to turn back. They refused. As many disobedients dropped to their knees to pray, Connor shouted to his officers, "Dammit. Turn on the hoses." The officers did not respond. In the intervening silence, the marchers stood as a group, moving forward. Connor's men, "as though hypnotized," fell back to allow them to proceed.[86]

It is difficult to say why the officers did not turn the fire hoses on the demonstrators or why Connor, whose virulent racism was well known, did not attempt to prevent the demonstrators from proceeding by himself. Did the number of demonstrators cow the officers into compliance? Was the crucial factor the crowd's determined and righteous bearing? Or was it that the officers could not subject a crowd dressed in their Sunday best to the indignity of fire hoses? Were the officers halted by the presence of reporters and cameras?

As King recounts it in "Black and White Together," the march to Ellsberry Park was preceded by an equally remarkable swing in the attitude of southern whites in Birmingham. Whites were not actively resisting the civil rights campaign as they had in the past.[87] Moreover, a percep-

[84] As well as a show of support for those arrested, the march was also prompted by the arrest of two activists, Guy and Candy Carawan, on the steps of the Sixteenth Street Baptist Church. Accounts differ on whether the march occurred shortly after 6 P.M. or 7 P.M. Hailey, "Birmingham Talks Pushed."

[85] Seeing the barricade, the demonstrators chanted "Turn on your water! Turn loose your dogs! We will stand here 'til we die!" Branch, *Parting the Waters*, 767. For additional accounts of the march, see Forman, *Making of Black Revolutionaries*, 312–16; Kunstler, *Deep in My Heart*, 190–94.

[86] King, *Why We Can't Wait*, 101. The *Birmingham World* reported a slightly different version of events: When the crowd approached the barricade, a leader of the movement, Wyatt Walker, held a "brief conference" with Connor. As a result, the "Police Commissioner motioned the marchers through." "Marchers Go Undoused in Sunday Demonstration."

[87] King, *Why We Can't Wait*, 100–101. The shift to a neutral stance among Birmingham whites was particularly significant because Birmingham was known for its antipathy toward civil rights. Angry local whites had openly attacked the Freedom Riders, for instance, while Birmingham police officers looked on. This long-standing and well-known antipathy was

tible change in attitude occurred within the African American community in Birmingham. The recruitment of volunteers who were willing to be arrested on behalf of the cause—a complicated task that had yielded uneven results—became markedly easier.[88] As King tells it, public opinion in Birmingham had shifted. His account suggests that the officers, sensing this shift, decided not to needlessly antagonize the movement. Was this change in public opinion the definitive factor? Again, it is difficult to say. If the accounts by sheriffs who encountered lynch mobs in post-Reconstruction South are a guide however, it seems likely that the march to Ellsberry Park turned out as it did due to a variety of factors. The officers were likely influenced by the size and dignified bearing of the crowd, as well as their perception (rightly or wrongly) of the prevailing public opinion. The Birmingham officers may have simply thought better of resisting a determined and upstanding crowd of two thousand that seemed to have public opinion on their side. What is clear, however, is that the authorities ceded an important victory to the demonstrators.

Because of its historical connections with the injustice and violence of the post-Reconstruction South, the victory of the civil rights movement at the march to Ellsberry Park is both praiseworthy and troubling. Given the South's history of slavery, racial hatred, black codes, Jim Crow laws, and, of course, lynching, the march seems like an unequivocal triumph of justice over injustice. And yet the connections between the Ellsberry victory and public lynch mobs should, I think, give us pause.

My point is not that civil and uncivil disobedience are indistinguishable. There are differences. Still, as I argued in the previous chapter, these differences are less obvious than one might initially suppose. Note that in the actual moment of the disobedience, it is particularly difficult to draw distinctions between civil and uncivil groups. While most Americans today understand that the civil rights protesters had a just cause, this was not as clear at the time. If it had been, the civil rights struggle would have been less of a struggle. It is also apparent in retrospect that the civil rights movement successfully maintained its commitment to nonviolent tactics. Yet as events were unfolding, the group's allegiance to nonviolence was

---

part of the reason that the city was chosen by the leadership of the civil rights movement. Klarman, *From Jim Crow to Civil Rights*, 433. As King put it, "If we can crack Birmingham, I am convinced we can crack the South. Birmingham is a symbol of segregation for the entire South." "Marchers Go Undoused in Sunday Demonstration."

[88] For much of the Birmingham campaign, the leadership had a difficult time recruiting volunteers who were willing to be arrested. This changed, however, when the movement focused its attention on young African Americans in Birmingham. Branch, *Parting the Waters*, 756–802; King, *Why We Can't Wait*, 96–109. The march to Ellsberry Park, for instance, was preceded by three days of protests in which more than one thousand individuals were arrested, many of them teenagers. The *New York Times* estimated that more than half of those arrested were under the age of eighteen. Hailey, "Birmingham Talks Pushed."

not entirely certain. Birmingham authorities feared violence from predominantly black crowds. Much of this fear was due to racist ideas of African American men as particularly prone to violent disorder. It is important to note, however, that fears about violence were not completely unfounded. Protesters had on occasion resorted to violence by throwing bricks and bottles at the authorities.[89] What's more, the issue of violence did fracture the movement as members who were dissatisfied with nonviolence broke off to form Black Power, an openly militant group.[90] This suggests both that the movement's commitment to nonviolence was hard won and that nonviolence was not a foreordained conclusion. It is plausible that the civil rights movement might have turned to violence, especially if its protests were not successful and its demands were unmet.

Vox Populi Redux

A particularly good way to see the differences between disobedients in the civil rights movement and public lynch mobs in the post-Reconstruction South is to focus on precisely the area that joins them: the normative view that the law should be connected to the morality of the people. Looking more closely at how each group understood the connection between morality and the law, some crucial differences emerge. In particular lynch mobs craved a tight, almost seamless relationship in which popular morality should govern law. Civil disobedients in the civil rights movement understood the relationship between their morality and the law as looser and more open. In their view, popular morality did not and should not always trump law. Indeed, sometimes law should govern and dominate morality.

This point is clarified by attending to the distinction between what H.L.A. Hart called duty-imposing rules and power-conferring rules.[91] Duty-imposing rules typically regulate the behavior of individuals. Through a system of incentives and punishments, duty-imposing rules obligate individuals to do various things such as stop at stop signs, pay taxes, register with Selective Service, and so on. Duty-imposing rules tell individuals what they are legally obligated to do (and forbidden from doing). Power-conferring rules explain how to identify, change, or enforce duty-imposing rules.[92] A power-conferring rule, for instance, explains how to resolve au-

[89] Branch, *Parting the Waters*, 758–60. Also see King, *Why We Can't Wait*, 104.

[90] On the centrality of the issue of violence in the split between Black Power and the civil rights movement, see Bosmajian and Bosmajian, *Rhetoric of the Civil-Rights Movement*, 19–32.

[91] Hart, *Concept of Law*, 91–93. Hart's distinction between duty-imposing rules and power-conferring rules has generated much debate. See Hacker and Raz, *Law, Morality, and Society*; and MacCormick, *H.L.A. Hart.*

[92] Hart, *Concept of Law*, 100–110.

thoritatively a dispute about whether a duty-imposing rule is valid. As such, power-conferring rules are directed toward government officials and administrators, rather than ordinary citizens, and define official practices and constitutional structures as opposed to governing individual behavior.

While King advocated violating duty-imposing rules (like, for instance, the statute in Birmingham that required a permit for a parade), he simultaneously argued that power-conferring rules must be obeyed. King's crucial argument on this point is that those who violate "an unjust law must do so openly, lovingly, and with a willingness to accept the punishment."[93] By submitting to official authority governing punishment, civil disobedients left power-conferring rules in tact. Civil disobedients did not believe they possessed the power to directly change or suspend the rules governing how duty-imposing rules were authoritatively identified, changed, or adjudicated, and, as such, they did not challenge the authority of government officials charged with punishing them. Civil disobedients in the civil rights movement understood power-conferring rules as a boundary on their action, and their concept of extralegal popular sovereignty was accordingly limited. This conceptual move is sharply at odds with lynch mobs.

To put this point differently, civil disobedients in the civil rights movement did not believe that power-conferring rules were a medium that could legitimately reflect their morality in a direct and unmediated fashion. King, it is important to note, was sharply critical of power-conferring rules and questioned the legitimacy and moral rectitude of officials charged with the task of authoritatively identifying, enforcing, and adjudicating duty-imposing rules. But critiquing of power-conferring rules is not the same thing as violating them, and criticizing legal officials is not the same as assuming their responsibilities.

The lynching crowds that killed Hose and Owens, in contrast, wanted to correct all the law's moral failings, and this perfectionist turn took them into the realm of violating power-conferring rules. They not only expressed their moral vision of what the law should do, they did it. For these lynch mobs, punishment and, by extension law, should look *just* so. This exactitude suggests the need for coherence between the ideal and the real, the normative and the empirical. For lynching crowds, the way to make the ideal real was through an expansive notion of popular power that extended to power-conferring rules. It is important to note that encroaching on power-conferring rules also may have eased the path to violence. Given the idea that the people can rightfully take on the duties of legal officials, the notion that the people can legitimately take on a predominant means of enforcement by legal officials—that is, violence—may logically follow.

[93] King, *Why We Can't Wait*, 83.

It is worth noting that King's reticence to exert direct moral control over power-conferring rules was coupled with a normative view of lawmaking as encompassing disagreement and conflict. King's *Letter from Birmingham Jail* suggests that no one true moral vision—his or any one else's—should dominate at the level of legislation. In the *Letter*, King is critical of the existing legislative process because it has tended to shut out dissenting voices and different views of morality. He draws attention to the injustice of a "numerical or power" majority making laws for the minority that do not apply to the majority (i.e., segregation statutes). King critiques of the legislative process in which a majority is able to force its morality on the minority because of an imbalance of power. Emphasizing this critique of moral homogeneity, King also attacks legislatures in which a minority has no part in enacting or devising laws because it is denied the right to vote. "Who can say," King pointedly asked, "that the legislature of Alabama which set up that state's segregation laws was democratically elected?"[94] A just legislative process, by implication, is one that allows for a political minority to participate in elections and to give voice to its own view of the political and moral issues of the day.[95] It consists of multiple voices on the moral questions of the day and conflicting points of view, not just that of the majority. As he emphasized elsewhere in the *Letter*, King did not shy from tension and conflict between groups, but rather saw these as productive means of change. "I must confess," he wrote, "that I am not afraid of the word 'tension.' . . . there is a type of constructive, nonviolent tension which is necessary for growth."[96]

The contrast with public lynch mobs is striking. Lynch mobs operated with a comparatively naturalized view of the community. They never

[94] Ibid.

[95] Though King posits that there is a relationship between the inclusiveness of the legislative process and justice of the resulting laws, he is vague about some crucial contours of this relationship. Given the context in which the *Letter* was written and its immediate aims, this is not surprising. Still, it is worth pointing out some remaining questions. It is not clear from the *Letter* what sort of minority participation in the legislature is necessary to make the legislative process inclusive. Would an inclusive process only require that minority citizens be able to vote for representatives? Would it require that minority candidates actually win seats in the legislature?

Also, it is not clear if King thought the exclusion of the minority party from the legislative process necessarily resulted in unjust laws. This would mean that the Thirteenth, Fourteenth, and Fifteenth Amendments to the Constitution were unjust and, even more bizarrely, that the Civil Rights Act of 1964 and the Voting Rights Act of 1965 were unjust. Nor is it clear from the *Letter* whether the opposite was true—that is, would an inclusive legislative process necessarily produce just laws? For instance, would a segregation law that the minority participated in making—and perhaps even assented to—be just? If an inclusive legislative process necessarily results in just laws, then, according to King's criteria, this segregation law would be just.

[96] King, *Why We Can't Wait*, 79.

asked how "they" had been constituted as a group or considered that different groups might have divergent perspectives to offer of moral truth. The mass lynch mob that killed Hose went to great efforts to make the community appear as a single, united force. In this case the desire for a homogeneous community even trumped a particularly enduring and pernicious division in the South: race. Recall, for instance, the report in the *Atlanta Constitution* that segments of the black community in Milner, Georgia, were, like their white counterparts, making every effort to catch Hose. If segments of the black community of Milner questioned the moral conviction of whites that Hose was guilty, the *Constitution* chose to ignore this division. This oversight was typical. Public lynch mobs and their defenders assumed over and over again that every moral, upstanding member of the community should be united in loathing the offender's "crimes" and in supporting vigilante violence. In their view, there was no other moral position on the matter. Objecting to the mob was tantamount to rejecting morality, shunning a communal notion of honor, inviting discord and disagreement into the community, and weakening communal bonds.

For King, in contrast, the polity was fragmented. There was a group with power and a group without it; a group historically at the center of lawmaking and a group at its margins; a group that traditionally defined justice in its own terms and a group whose moral perspective had been silenced. This assumption of divisions within the political community is, I think, related to King's attention to power-conferring rules that provide a mechanism for resolving disputes about what constitutes legitimate duty-imposing rules and how these rules can be introduced, eliminated, or changed. Power-conferring rules become important in light of divisions, not in the absence of them. If everyone agrees about the right thing to do, then rules that prescribe how to work out differences are superfluous. If, to put the point differently, the collective moral sentiment of the community is simply "out there" waiting to be expressed, then it is not necessary to ask freedmen and -women living in Milner, Georgia, in 1899 about the justice of Hose's actions. What could they say that would matter? In contrast, King's framework suggests that the freedmen and -women of Milner would have something to say about the justice of punishing Hose, and, as a disempowered group, their perspective would likely be distinct from that of the majority. And, justice could require that this minority group be permitted to speak and, ideally, be heard.

Freedmen and -women living in the post-Reconstruction South often wryly observed that the criminal-justice system did not live up to its name. Justice in the South, so a saying went, meant "just us." Unable to serve on juries and largely absent from the ranks of judges, lawyers, and sheriffs, freedmen and -women did not have an active and participatory role in formal legal proceedings. The formal legal system silenced them. The same might be said of extralegal violence in the post-Reconstruction South. Though populist in spirit, public lynch mobs were not inclusive in their normative understanding of law or morality. Justice outside of the courts meant "just us" too.

The civil rights movement's conception of the relationship between law and morality was not "just us." Its approach to power-conferring laws makes this clear. For it, moral disagreement was everywhere, within the movement and outside of it. Moreover, the movement's normative stance was that difference and disagreement should not be resisted out of hand but rather accepted and negotiated. It is important to note that the movement's conflictual view of morality did not imply an apathetic approach to politics or moral relativism. Multiple perspectives on morality did not, in other words, mean anything goes. Nor did it mean that no correct answer to the moral questions facing the country could be found. King and others in the civil rights movement clearly possessed strong normative ideas about the law, and they were not reticent about asserting their views. At the same time, they did not assume that others should necessarily agree with their convictions. Indeed, King's *Letter* suggests that disagreements about morality could be a creative and productive force in law, not a problem to be solved.

Delving into the historical record of lynching violence provides a deeper appreciation of the appeal of a naturalized and homogeneous conception of popular morality. Lynch mobs wanted the people to be powerful and decisive and, like a mighty popular leviathan, capable of crushing those who stood in its way, be they alleged offenders or legal officials. As they saw it, unanimity about moral truths enabled commanding and resolute action. To refer back to the image offered by one apologist of a giant swatting a mosquito, it is difficult to imagine the giant acting (let alone acting in such a way that inspires fear and commands respect) if he is of two minds as to the appropriate moral response to the mosquito. As lynching crowds imagined it, their popular leviathan was always of one mind on the "correct" moral action. And, this view on the positive relationship between action and moral cohesion does raise a question as to how the civil rights movement was able to accept moral disagreement within the group and to act collectively. One might wonder how it was able to pull off embracing moral dissension within its own ranks. It is clearer, however, why the civil rights movement adopted a morally pluralistic approach, as it would have had difficulty with the image of the mighty popular leviathan that erased the plurality inherent in the human condition. It understood, instead, that popular groups are composed of many minds and are typically *of* many minds on moral issues.

Chapter Four

MILITANT ABOLITIONISTS

MORALITY—OR, MORE PRECISELY, the sharp jab of a perceived injustice that brings cries of violation, rights, and fairness to the fore—has had an uneasy relationship with civic participation in democratic politics. During the rise of modern democracy, morality certainly was a boon to participation, leading radicals and revolutionaries to challenge unjust rulers and illegitimate forms of government. It is difficult to imagine accounting for the success of democratic revolutions without addressing the capacity of moral claims to prompt individuals to act politically.

This complementary relationship between morality and democracy is complicated, however, by the American abolitionist movement, whose history reveals an unexpected switch: Morality can lead to political withdrawal and to an inward-looking absorption in the moral worth of the individual. This was an odd development, to be sure. The abolitionists, in particular the immediatist branch of the movement, had an explicitly political agenda, and what's more, their political goals were other-regarding to the point of altruism. How did their selfless, activist political agenda become reversed? What would lead a group that articulated and embodied many ideals of participatory democracy to eventually encourage its members to act as politically inert lumps?

Part of this switch concerns Socrates' conundrum about how to be a moral individual in an immoral polity and, more specifically, the problem of dirty hands.[1] Abolitionists questioned whether they should pay taxes to governments that sustained slavery, and they wondered whether they should wear cotton or drink their tea with sugar, both of which supported a slave economy. They asked whether they should vote, even for abolitionist candidates. They thought carefully about how obedience to state, federal, and constitutional laws that allowed for and maintained the enslavement of men and women might well imperil their souls.

Some abolitionists chose resistance and, like vigilantes and lynch mobs, defied the law by conducting fugitive slave rescues.[2] Many immediatist

[1] Walzer, "Political Action." For more on the problem of dirty hands in abolitionist thought, see Ellis, *Dark Side of the Left*, 17–43; and Young, *Reconsidering American Liberalism*, 107–25.

[2] On abolitionist violence, see Friedman, *Wise Minority*, 28–50; Grimsted, *American Mobbing*, 33–82; McKivigan and Harold, *Antislavery Violence*, 1–37. On the appeal of

abolitionists opted out of politics and, in direct contrast with the populist zeal of vigilantes and lynch mobs, chose not to act politically on their steadfast and unerring moral conviction that slavery was an intolerable evil. The immediatists' were appalled and pained at the injustice of the law. Yet their strong moral convictions counterintuitively led to an overwrought sense of legal obligation and to political withdrawal. Their example indicates that zealous action, violence, and radical autonomy are not the only potential hazards of robust moral convictions about the injustice of the law. Inaction, passivity, and utter domination are as well.

Another group of abolitionists, the radical political abolitionists, reveals a third approach that attempted to situate itself between violent disobedience and passive obedience. Radicals searched, tentatively and unsteadily, to acknowledge moral autonomy as well as obedience to law. They were not entirely successful and, like vigilantes and lynch mobs, tended to emphasize freedom from law and the necessity of violent means. Yet, unlike these groups, radicals did engage with the Constitution, an act that gestures to a paradoxical union of autonomy from law and subjection to law. Their example is also intriguing because it takes place in a noninstitutional setting. It does not involve showdowns with sheriffs, break-ins to jails, or storming courts of law. Through them, it is possible to think about the tension between democracy and constitutionalism at a different register, that is, beyond institutions and legal officials.

Political Beginnings

To understand the immediatists' political withdrawal, it is essential to understand the political and legal struggles that preceded it.[3] The abolitionist movement was long-lived, stretching from the early days of the republic to the Civil War, and its changing attitudes toward morality and the law were bound up with persistent frustrations over the pace and extent

---

mob action and the value of rational argument in the antebellum period, see Smith, *Dominion of Voice*, 11–83.

[3] This background is essential because, as Mika LaVaque-Manty observes, principles of political action depend on context. He writes:

> [N]o agent can have a complete set of absolute principles as a practical guide. To think that an agent has a ready and straightforward blueprint for what to do in pursuit of her principles is to ignore that (1) the principles need a social context for their realization and, that is always contingent, and (2) the meaning of the blueprint also depends on the social context. . . . there are no principles that fully predate actual justificatory practices. (LaVaque-Manty, *Arguments and Fists*, 170).

of substantive political change.[4] The abolitionists' understanding of the law shifted dramatically over the course of nearly a century. Gradualists, immediatists, and radical political abolitionists did not agree, for instance, on whether citizens had to obey unjust laws, on whether the law could be a productive force of change, or on how to interpret the slave clauses of the Constitution. Nor did they agree on how to bring about political change.

These debates and disagreements were prompted by two facts that dogged the abolitionists: They sharply disagreed with federal, state, and constitutional laws that supported slavery and they had little chance of changing these laws through the standard political channels because they were a political minority, a fringe movement. Northern abolitionists opposed local laws that either explicitly or tacitly supported slavery as well as federal laws, like the Fugitive Slave Acts of 1793 and 1850, and the slave provisions of the Constitution.[5] Four parts of the Constitution were at issue because they either recognized or supported slavery: the three-fifths clause, which apportioned Congressional representation and direct taxation according to the number of citizens and three fifths "of all other persons"; the provision in Article I, section 9, which permitted the international importation and trade of slaves until 1808; the fugitive slave clause; and the provisions in Article I and Article IV permitting the federal government to suppress internal insurrections, including slave revolts. The idea that free states were bound to return escaped slaves to bondage or that one's government might legitimately suppress slaves battling for freedom was particularly galling to the abolitionists. Because of these provisions, individual abolitionists felt they were morally bound up with the wickedness of slavery; they were caught up in and constricted by its evil.

What's more, because they were a political minority, the American political system was not kind to the abolitionists. Indeed, their political travails serve as a perverse testament to the success of Madison's goal in *The Federalist*, no. 10 to temper the effects of factions, the "moral disease under which popular governments have everywhere perished." As Madison suggested, the abolitionists did find that it was "more difficult for all who feel" a common cause "to discover their own strength, and to act in

[4] On the course and changing tactics of the abolitionist struggle, see Barnes, *The Antislavery Impulse*; Davis, *Problem of Slavery in the Age of Revolution*; Davis, *The Problem of Slavery in Western Culture*; Dumond, *Antislavery*; Elkins, *Slavery*; Filler, *Crusade against Slavery*; Kraditor, *Means and Ends in American Abolitionism*; Newman, *Transformation of American Abolitionism*; Perry, *Radical Abolitionism*; Sewell, *Ballots for Freedom: Antislavery Politics in the United States*. On the abolitionists after 1856, see McPherson, *Abolitionist Legacy*.

[5] Cover, *Justice Accused*; Friedman, *Wise Minority*; Kraditor, *Means and Ends in American Abolitionism*; Wiecek, *Sources of Antislavery Constitutionalism in America*.

unison with each other" in a vast country that took in "a greater variety of parties and interests." National stability tended to win out over justice during most of the life of the movement. And yet remarkably the abolitionists persisted in their cause with incredible determination.[6]

The first attempt at addressing offensive laws and unfriendly politics undertaken by the gradualists was elitist and homeopathic. The gradualists were a choice group composed of philanthropists, renowned businessmen and lawyers, and political representatives, and their efforts were directed toward others like them. In a clubby political world, a political minority was not necessarily disadvantaged, and thus they courted political representatives, Madison's "chosen . . . citizens," whose "wisdom may best discern the true interest of their country, and whose patriotism and love of justice will be least likely to sacrifice it to temporary or partial interests." For gradualists, the way to address unjust law and politics was *through* law and politics. The Pennsylvania Abolition Society, a hub of early efforts, exemplified of this approach. Benjamin Franklin was the group's first president, and Benjamin Rush, Noah Webster, Elbridge Gerry, General Lafayette, and Granville Sharp were associated with it as well. The group sent over twenty petitions to Congress and over forty petitions to the Pennsylvania legislature before 1830;[7] they brought legal cases forward, both to represent fugitive slaves and to ensure that the state laws protecting free blacks were interpreted favorably; they looked for every legal loophole; they cajoled and negotiated backroom political deals.

Accompanying the early movement's attention to institutional politics was at least a whiff of noblesse oblige. The early movement, for the most part, was not racially integrated, and, as was generally the case throughout the movement, gradualist abolitionists gave little thought to developing institutional structures that would facilitate the transition of African Americans to freedom.[8] Abolition itself was sufficient. And, at points, abolition seemed more an opportunity to commend white generosity than to underscore the legitimacy of the rights of slaves. The authors of the Pennsylvania Act for the Gradual Abolition of Slavery in 1780, for instance, noted that they had the "particular blessing . . . to add one more

[6] Kaminski and Leffler, *Federalists and Antifederalists*, 26–32. As James Morone notes, the Second Great Awakening played a crucial role in sustaining the abolitionists because it "restored an early American vision—the city on the hill, a mission to the entire world. Reformers mixed the biblical millennium with republican ferment. . . . The moral dreams inspired what we would now call a powerful social movement with vast institutional consequences." Morone, *Hellfire Nation*, 142.

[7] For a fuller discussion of the political petitions of the gradualist movement, see Filler, *Crusade against Slavery*, 10–27; Newman, *Transformation of American Abolitionism*, 16–60.

[8] Elkins, *Slavery*. For a critique of Elkins, see Kraditor, *Means and Ends in American Abolitionism*.

step to universal civilization, by removing as much as possible the sorrows of those who have lived in such undeserved bondage." Given the success of the American Revolution, they went on, "we find our hearts enlarged with kindness and benevolence towards men in all conditions and nations; and we conceive ourselves at this particular period extraordinarily called upon by the blessings which we have received, to maintain the sincerity of our profession, and to give substantial proof of our gratitude."[9] Unlike the *Germantown Friends' Protest against Slavery* in 1688, which asked plainly whether slaves had "not as much right to fight for their freedom as you have to keep them slaves" or James Otis's firm pronouncement in "The Rights of the British Colonies Asserted and Approved" that "those who barter away other men's liberty will soon care little for their own," the Pennsylvania Act speaks of benevolence, generosity, and blessings.[10] Liberty, like an unexpected windfall, was something that should be passed on to the less fortunate.

Other gradualists in favor of colonization were less sanguine about the capacity of government to accommodate freedom for both whites and blacks. Signaling early doubts about the effectiveness of institutional politics to adequately address the social and moral dimensions of slavery, the American Colonization Society raised funds to transport freeborn blacks and emancipated slaves to the west coast of Africa and to assist with the establishment of local institutions such as churches and schools. It was hoped that these colonies, as exporters of camwood, ivory, palm oil, tortoise shell, and gold, would become self-sufficient and free. Beneath this optimism were deep-seated doubts about racial equality. As one advocate urged, "Let us look into our own hearts. Let us listen to the silent though powerful voice of nature, and ask ourselves if she does not forbid our union with blacks."[11] Tocqueville reached a similar conclusion and also supported colonization. Though Tocqueville described the racial manners and mores of white society as based on an "imaginary inequality," he stressed the difficulty of achieving racial equality. While the "the legal barrier which separated the two races is tending to fall away," that "which exists in the manners of the country" was not. Indeed, prejudice against blacks "appears to be stronger in the States which have abolished slavery, than in those where it still exists; and nowhere is it so intolerant as in those states where servitude has never been known." Tocqueville was doubtful that significant racial violence could be avoided in the United

[9] The Act also placed blame for slavery on Britain, a country that offered "no effectual, legal relief" for human bondage. It is reprinted in Pennsylvania Society for Promoting the Abolition of Slavery, *Constitution*, 8–9.

[10] Society of Friends, *Germantown Friends' Protest against Slavery*. Otis, *Some Political Writings of James Otis*, 66.

[11] *Colonizationist and Journal of Freedom*, 102.

States. He offered tepid support for colonization, claiming that it "may have the effect of changing the fate of a portion of the human race."[12]

True to the ethos of gradualism, discretion was the watchword among advocates of colonization. "We cannot go, we have no right to go, directly to the slave and tear off his fetters," Horace Mann asserted in a speech to the Young Men's Colonization Society in 1833. Mann reasoned that the reach of abolition was necessarily limited because slave-holding states were "to us like *foreign States*." The solution to this lack of jurisdiction or influence was diplomacy toward slave owners: "We can alienate their feelings until they become foreign enemies; or, on the other hand, we can conciliate them until they become allies and auxiliaries in the sacred cause of emancipation."[13] A conciliatory approach, for some, came close to an enabling one. As critics pointed out, colonization was a boon to the slave owners because it rid them of surplus population; the old and the handicapped could be freed and sent to the Grand Basa tract or Monrovia, thus relieving masters of this financial burden. And on a more general note of dissatisfaction with gradualism, the charge was made that an appeasing, conciliatory approach gutted abolition of one of its most forceful attacks on slavery: moral outrage.

Theory of Moral Complicity and the Death of Politics

By the 1830s a second wave of abolitionists generally identified with Garrison and David Walker adopted a markedly different approach to the political challenges presented by a large political agenda and small numbers.[14] The immediatists' response to their political conundrum was not to mollify their political message—just the opposite happened as the group adopted a far more strident, uncompromising tone. And to boost the size of the group, the movement courted ordinary individuals instead of politicians.[15] In large measure, their strategy of mass appeal rested on making individuals feel complicit in the wickedness of the state and fed-

[12] Tocqueville, *Democracy in America*. In particular, see "Situation of the Black Population in the United States, and Dangers with which its Presence Threatens the Whites," (subsection in chap. xviii, vol. 1).

[13] *The Colonizationist and Journal of Freedom*, 12–17.

[14] There were many reasons for the development of immediatism, including revivalism, a more egalitarian political ethos, and the rising influence of freed black and female activists. For more on the development of immediatism, see Barnes, *The Antislavery Impulse*, 3–37; Dumond, *Antislavery*; Filler, *The Crusade against Slavery*, 28–107; Newman, *Transformation of American Abolitionism*, 86–130.

[15] Scholars are divided as to whether Garrison helped or harmed abolition. For negative appraisals of Garrison, see Barnes, *Antislavery Impulse*; Dumond, *Antislavery*; Thomas, *Liberator*. For more favorable assessments of Garrison, see Fanuzzi, *Abolition's Public Sphere*; Kraditor, *Means and Ends in American Abolitionism*; Perry, *Radical Abolitionism*.

eral government. Yet, these charges of complicity, which were perhaps more powerful than the immediatists understood, ran a strange course and were integral to the switch from political engagement to withdrawal.

In their political strategy and in some cases their demeanor, the immediatists were populists; they saw great potential in the power of the people. Thus, their appeals, petitions, and admonitions were directed toward the ordinary folks who, despite their good intentions, had failed to grasp the extent to which they were linked to the sins of slavery or had ignored the urgency of its threat to their moral worth. They concentrated on the many, reasoning that governing elites would not be able to resist the overwhelming force of a collective outcry against slavery.[16] And they focused on the heart. Urging every soul to listen to the internal voice of conscience, they believed along with Emerson that "every time a man goes back to his own thoughts . . . angels receive him, talk with him, and, that, in the best hours, he is uplifted in virtue of this essence, into a peace and power which the material world cannot give." Their object was to prompt reflection on the "greasy hotel" of political and social life that accommodated slavery and to encourage the sort of normative speculations that underscored just how compromised and compromising everyday life was.[17] Setting the emotional stage for Harriet Beecher Stowe's *Uncle Tom's Cabin*, immediatist abolitionists peered into the dark heart of every man and woman with the hopes of instigating a desire for pure and perfect metaphysical truth and revulsion toward the corruptions of institutional politics. Thus, they tended to agree with Max Weber that the "world is filled with demons and he who lets himself into politics . . . contracts with diabolical powers."[18] Unlike Weber, however, immediatist abolitionists saw little reason to enter into such a bargain at an institutional level. Instead they turned attention to the intimate habits and heart of the individual.

Though immediatism was hostile to institutional politics and was generally un-tethered from government, it was political, at least at first.[19] In its resolute grassroots campaign to spark widespread outrage in every

[16] Garrison summed up the strategy of moral suasion as

> [I]t is the grand object of the Anti-Slavery Society so to affect public sentiment, and touch the issues of religious and political action, and alter the views and feeling so the people in regard to the crime of slaveholding, that all classes of society, churchmen and politicians, law-makers and law-executioners, those who can use the elective franchise and those who cannot, may be induced to rally together, en masse, for the entire abolition of slavery. (Birney and Garrison, *Letter on the Political Obligations of Abolitionists*, 25)

[17] Emerson, *Emerson's Antislavery Writings*, 59.

[18] Weber, *Weber*, 362.

[19] For more on the anti-institutional tendencies of abolition and the tension between moral absolutes and tactical flexibility, see Perry, *Radical Abolitionism*.

person it could possibly reach, immediatism represented a different kind of political action. The immediatists' mission was to spark a conflagration, one individual, or one meeting, or one town at a time. The object was to "warm up . . . the people. . . . Our speeches, our publications, our Societies, our Conventions, our prayers are kindling up a sacred fire that shall cause the mind to glow . . . and our public servants to feel its warming influence."[20] Building on a newfound interest in the public sphere that arose during the Jacksonian era and the participatory flavor of religious revivalism, abolitionists instigated small-scale conversions to their cause through conventions, mass rallies, speaking campaigns, and a slew of new publications such as the *North Star*, the *Liberator*, and *Freedom's Journal*. Moreover, true to the professions of human equality and the grassroots tenor of their campaign, the movement's membership expanded to include former slaves and women. Noncitizens had a role to play too, the immediatists reasoned, in changing the morality of the nation.

In contrast to the quiet and conciliatory tone of gradualism, their moral outrage was central and explicit. The political disposition of immediatism was expressed most clearly in Garrison's opening shot in the *Liberator*: "I am in earnest—I will not equivocate—I will not excuse—I will not retreat a single inch—and I will be heard!" Arguing against the gradualist position that tiptoed around the feelings of slave owners, the American Anti-Slavery Society, the principal organization of immediatism, was explicit that slavery was an evil that could not be tolerated. "The supineness of New England on this subject," observed Lydia Marie Child, "reminds me of the man who was being asked to work at the pump, because the vessel was going down, [and who] answered, 'I am only a passenger.'"[21] Slavery was a calamity that not only involved those directly engaged in the enslavement of others but also implicated those who saw themselves as blameless. The goal of immediatist abolitionists was to make the imminent threat of the sinking ship of state so palpable that it could neither be dismissed nor wished away.

Yet, in terms of the biblical argument against slavery, convincing others of the moral wrong of slavery (let alone their role in it) was more com-

[20] Stanton, quoted in Newman, *Transformation of American Abolitionism*, 131. Garrison referred to the abolitionist task as "waking up the nation."

> The sea of agitation is rising higher and higher; the storm of excitement is increasing in power and sublimity; the land is reeling from the earthquake shocks of the conflicting moral elements. The abolition of slavery is the all-pervading subject of conversation, discussion, inquiry, and speculation, from one end of the country to the other. All political, all religious, all legislative bodies, are compelled to give it their serious attention, and to take some kind of action upon it. ("Progress of the Anti-Slavery Movement")

[21] Child, *Appeal in Favor of That Class of Americans Called Africans*, 133.

plex than might first be supposed. Pro-slavery interests were quick to point out that a close reading of the Bible, especially the Mosaic code of the Old Testament, suggested that slavery was a morally acceptable practice.[22] Leviticus 25, for instance, provides guidelines to the Hebrews for the enslavement of "heathens" (as opposed to brethren), indicating, among other things, how slaves should be purchased and bequeathed. Apologists for slavery also relied heavily on the Paul's Epistle of Philemon, arguing that it provided an admirable example of the capture and return of a runaway slave. Immediatists countered these specific references creatively (presaging the radical political abolitionists' resourceful interpretations of the slave provisions of the Constitution), but their most forceful scriptural appeal was altogether different. It was general, not specific. The pervasive message of the New Testament, they argued, was kindness, love, and equality, and the commandment that "Thou shalt love thy neighbor as thyself" indicated a moral condemnation of slavery. Immediatists maintained that treating a slave well—as one might want to be treated if enslaved—was not enough, and instead the commandment indicated that the force and oppression necessary to maintain slavery violated natural, human equality.

If the immediatists were relatively successful at keeping biblical arguments in the movement, they were less successful at keeping institutional politics, law, and the Constitution out of it. First, the membership, riled up by the moving rhetoric of peripatetic firebrands, wanted to know how they could halt slavery both in the South and in the new territories, and, second, fights over slavery were increasingly a part of institutional politics. Beginning with the Missouri Compromise in 1820, the slavery question was revisited in 1846 during discussions of the Wilmot Proviso and again in 1854 when Stephen Douglas successfully guided the Kansas-Nebraska Act through Congress. The press of formal politics was also spurred by the immediatists' focus on individual complicity. To be complicit is to establish a connection between the acts of the government and the soul of the individual, as well as between the external and the internal and the guilty and the innocent. Complicity is a partnership; it renders one an accomplice in a crime. Given the underlying legal metaphor, it is perhaps not too surprising that immediatist abolitionists began to think more about government, law, and the Constitution. And they understood the law not as a homeopathic means to a cure, as the gradualists had, but rather as a conduit of evil and a tie to the morally fetid South. To the immediatists, complicity did imply a partnership, but it was one

[22] Shanks, "Biblical Anti-Slavery Argument of the Decade." Also see Phillips, *Constitution a Pro-Slavery Compact*, 104. On the political and religious context that preceded abolition, see Wyatt-Brown, "Prelude to Abolitionism."

they wanted no part of. Thus, an idea and strategy that originated in order to establish bonds between free Americans and the enslaved millions in the South and to foster a sense of responsibility among sympathetic northerners for those in bondage ended in dreams of severance and renunciation.

A question that prompted this reversal was: Could an abolitionist in good conscience vote? This question no doubt sounds strange to a contemporary political observer attuned to a pragmatic approach to politics. Of course abolitionists should have voted, casting their ballots for local, state, and federal representatives who were most closely allied with abolitionist goals. A grassroots strategy does not preclude a more formal method of change. For immediatists however, these strategies were distinct. Voting raised the issue of complicity in a way that moral suasion did not because it established a direct line of agreement and authority between the individual and the government.[23] In the most extreme version of this argument, voting was understood to authorize the government to act and to legitimate its actions, which in turn tainted the voter with its wickedness. Thus,

> each voter is the Congress, the President, the commander-in-chief, the constable, jailor and hangman; the army and the navy; and when . . . the fugitive slave [is] taken back in chains and tears; the slave-trade carried on; the slaves shot down for doing what the nation declares is "obedience to God;" these deeds are done by the two and a half millions of voters; and each voter is principle in these acts of villainy and outrage. Each voter breaks all the necks that are broken by the government; and does all the shooting and stabbing done by it.[24]

Understood as agents of the voters, political representatives—and more specifically their deeds—bore as much weight on the moral standing of abolitionists as on their own actions. By voting, abolitionists did not merely condone the government's crimes or abet the government in them. Rather, it was as if abolitionists committed these atrocities themselves. If each voter *was* the Congress, then each act of the Congress was the act of the voter.

Abolitionists spun out this idea as far as it could go and farther, claiming moral responsibility for the actions of those they had not elected

[23] Voting was not the only issue faced by immediatists, who also worried about the complicity implied by paying taxes to the government, using money coined by the government, doing business with banks and insurance companies chartered by the government, testifying in the government's courts of law, and even signing abolitionist petitions to Congress. See Perry, *Radical Abolitionism*, 77–80.

[24] Ballou, "Address." Also see Phillips, "No-Voting Theory"; Wright, "Ballot-Box and Battlefield."

(jailors and hangmen) or did not exert much direct control over (the army and navy). But if they were overeager in their examples, the political difficulty that they struck on was sound. How much control should voters have over their legal and political representatives? How much were citizens in a representative democracy morally culpable for the actions of their government officials? And more puzzling still, what was the moral culpability of a citizen who voted for the losing candidate? If he or she was still represented by the winner (as we commonly suppose), then was she or he morally responsible for what the winner stood for too? Hobbes provided one answer to this question in his assertion that political control between sovereign and subjects flowed in only one direction. Once subjects had authorized the sovereign, they could not weasel out of this agreement or be freed from their political obligation. Their control began and ended with the act of authorization itself, in other words.[25] Under this model, the abolitionists had little to worry about; their vote authorized political and legal officials but did not imply any control once those officials were in office and, by extension, presumably did not imply any moral culpability for their actions either.

The immediatists took a different approach and assumed that democratic government ideally implied a one-to-one relationship with those carrying out their will: Voter and government were so closely bound that the wishes and conscience of one and the acts of the other would be indistinguishable. This idea is elucidated particularly well by frontier vigilantes, discussed in chapter 2, who emphasize a seamless relationship between the sovereign and the government. These vigilantes underscored that the sovereign people made the law while the government merely executed sovereign will through the enforcement of the law. To them, the government was a functionary, having borrowed and subordinated life and living in the shadow of those they serve.

For the abolitionists, this dream of a "government as instrument of will" fueled their conviction that they were living in a dystopia. If the government and the people were ideally bonded together in an integral relationship, then what were the implications of the government going morally astray? As the immediatists saw it, citizens would go astray too. Voting meant that their moral worth was as bound to the contemptible laws and policies of their government as the "North is bound together with the South, a living body with the dead carcass of slavery, and the blood of our life well nigh curdled in our veins by the portentous conjecture."[26] Given this choice, voting looked less like an act of freedom and more like a bargain with the devil. Thus, Adin Ballou concluded that he

[25] Hobbes, *Leviathan*, part II, chap. xviii.

[26] Browne, "Speech at the Anniversary of the New York Young Men's Anti-Slavery Society."

would not vote, even if his single vote would accomplish the one thing that immediatist abolitionists most fervently desired: the immediate abolition of slavery.[27] Ballou's statement was intended to highlight the self-defeating quality of voting for a corrupted government, but more importantly it reveals a larger self-defeating turn in the abolitionist movement. Fear of complicity had trumped the goal of abolition, and individual responsibility for the well-being of one's own soul superseded a shared responsibility for the well-being of the enslaved.

Underneath this fear of complicity was an assumption that their representative agents *would* go astray and fail the moral duty of the abolitionists. Yet, on the face of it, this assumption makes little sense. It is not clear why officials would consistently act immorally on the slavery question. According to the immediatists, the Constitution itself foreordained this evil. Politicians, swearing in their oath of office to support and defend the Constitution, pledged their support for the provisions that explicitly and implicitly supported slavery. This support, once given, was binding; there was no way around it. In a similar way, voters pledged themselves completely to the Constitution by voting: ". . . to be a qualified citizen I must be under an oath of allegiance to the Constitution. I must be a consenting party to it. I must bind myself to abide by it as a rule of my political practice."[28] Thus, immediatists believed that the Constitution had a clear, unambiguous meaning—it was, as its authors intended, a pro-slavery pact—and that an oath to it was an affirmation of the principle of slavery as much as it was an affirmation of any other constitutional provision. The Constitution "*means precisely what those who framed it and adopted it meant*—NOTHING MORE, NOTHING LESS as a matter of bargain and compromise. . . . No just or honest use of it can be made, in opposition to the plain intention of its framers, *except to declare the contract at an end, and to refuse to serve under it.*"[29] Given this, two moral choices presented themselves: One could opt out of politics and citizenship, becoming instead a "mere subject," or one could attempt to violently bring down the regime.[30] For the most part, immediatists, particularly white immediatists, remained steadfastly opposed to the use of force in any human relationship. Some went so far as to argue that slave insurrections were illegitimate. Thus, a core group chose to opt out rather than to fight.

Bolstering this decision, immediatists argued that to interpret the Constitution outside the parameters of original intent amounted to fraud

[27] Ballou, "Address."

[28] Ibid. Also see "Constitutionality of Slavery"; Phillips, *Review of Lysander Spooner's Essay on the Unconstitutionality of Slavery*; Phillips, *Constitution a Pro-Slavery Compact.*

[29] Phillips, *The Constitution a Pro-Slavery Compact*, 96. Emphasis original. On the issue of amendments, also see "Liberty Party Defined."

[30] Ballou, "Address." On disunion, also see Browne, "Speech"; "Gerrit Smith's Constitutional Argument No. Iii"; "Liberty Party Defined"; Phillips, "No-Voting Theory."

toward the pro-slavery interests that had agreed to it. To interpret the Constitution as something other than a pro-slavery compact was, in other words, to renege on a promise much as a con man or a libertine might disavow earlier pledges and oaths. The abolitionists, righteous and honorable, would not engage in this dishonesty, even to promote a worthy end. Thus, polar opposites were rendered the same to them: The northern member of Congress who won on an abolitionist campaign was no different from the southern member of Congress who won on a pro-slavery campaign. By virtue of their shared oath to uphold the Constitution, they were the same. Narrowing the meaning of each politician's oath of office to the Constitution even further, they discounted the prospect of amendment almost entirely. The politician taking the oath of office or the citizen voting "is to take [the Constitution] *as it is*, not *as it may be*. It *may be* amended for the better, or for the worse—that is not the question. What is it NOW?"[31] Thus, at every turn, immediatists shut down the possibility of constitutional change. The document was wholly binding as written and offered two choices: One could join in its pro-slavery cause or secede from it.

Because of their conviction that ordinary and constitutional laws were absolutely binding on officials and citizens, immediatist abolitionists have been referred to as positivists.[32] In many respects this designation makes sense. They held that the law, no matter how unjust or morally reprehensible, was valid law. In other words, laws need not replicate morality or satisfy moral claims to be bone fide laws. In other respects, however, the label of positivism is a strange one. Immediatists did not accept that these valid laws merited their obedience, as Austin and Bentham would have it. A concern of early legal positivists was to dissuade citizens from making hasty decisions about the law's validity. Positivism serves stability. If unjust laws are posited to be valid and to command obedience, then the legitimacy of the existing government is aided, if not assured.[33]

For the immediatists, however, utter obedience did not lead to stability and peace. For some, obedience to law demanded their exit from the legal and political system.[34] The result of their positivism was not political

[31] "Liberty Party Defined." Phillips, *Constitution a Pro-Slavery Compact*, 108. Emphasis original.

[32] Cover, *Justice Accused*, 1–30 and 149–91; Wiecek, *Sources of Antislavery Constitutionalism in America*, 228–48.

[33] As Hart points out, it takes both these propositions (law is valid and law is to be obeyed) to ensure stability. If laws are understood to be valid and to be *unjust*, then unrest like civil disobedience is possible. See "Law and Morals," in Hart, *Concept of Law*, 185–212.

[34] Exiting the political system was particularly dramatic for those who had official roles in it. For Massachusetts justice of the peace Francis Jackson, for instance, a departure from law and politics meant resigning his position. Explaining his decision, he noted that the Constitution "is dead to me, and I to it." Phillips, *Constitution a Pro-Slavery Compact*, 119.

constancy, but quietism and escapism as a form of resistance. Immediatism created a class of political Bartleby the Scriveners, who "preferred not to" be accomplices to the existing regime and hoped that a growing group of "mere subjects" might fell their pro-slavery government. The intent of opting out of politics was defiance and resistance, not appeasement. Indeed, the immediatists derided appeasement by, for instance, attacking William Paley and the reduction of moral obligation to expediency.[35] Immediatists demanded a new regime, "a strong, a righteous, a perfect government . . . which is of heaven, not of men." They sought a government "administered by an infallible Judge, an impartial Lawgiver, the King of kings, and Lord of lords."[36] The contrast with the existing government and its founding document—which Garrison regularly referred to as a "covenant with death and an agreement with hell"[37]—could not be more explicit.

For others, like John Brown, complete obedience to unjust laws was unacceptable. With no middle ground and no way to think about how to resist and to obey, more extreme steps seemed necessary. Unwilling to fully obey and reluctant to passively live in an unjust political regime, some understood the only option as violent, wholesale change. Given the corner they found themselves in, it is perhaps not too surprising that some individuals within the movement eventually rejected the group's long-standing adherence to pacifism. All that was necessary to prompt the likes of John Brown was the belief that God's revolutionary work required action, even violent action, and that to do otherwise would mean being complicit in an unjust regime. One extreme seemed to justify another.[38]

For those who continued to refuse violence, the idea of complicity had reduced a grassroots political movement full of agitation and zeal to a group of political mutes who dreamed of escaping their current bonds. Even Thoreau, who admonished his fellow citizens to "Cast your whole vote, not a strip of paper merely, but your whole influence," dreamed of a social contract that would afford him an escape from government. "I please myself with imagining a state . . . which even would not think it inconsistent with its own repose, if a few were to live aloof from it, not

[35] Paley, *Principles of Moral and Political Philosophy.*

[36] Birney and Garrison, *Letter on the Political Obligations of Abolitionists*, 16. Garrison also wrote, "Human governments are to be viewed as judicial punishment." "Prospectus of the Liberator, Volume Viii."

[37] The reference is from Isaiah 28:14–18: "Therefore hear the word of the Lord, you scoffers, who rule this people in Jerusalem! Because you have said, 'We have made a covenant with death and with Sheol we have an agreement.' . . . Then your covenant with death will be annulled, and your agreement with Sheol will not stand; when the overwhelming scourge passes through you will be beaten down by it."

[38] Reynolds, *John Brown, Abolitionist.* On the cultural and political significance of John Brown's execution, see Nudelman, *John Brown's Body.*

meddling with it, nor embraced by it, who fulfilled all the duties of neighbors and fellow-men."[39] The fantasy of living aloof, a salve for the conscience, was poison for participatory democratic politics. Rather than using the full power they possessed as citizens to free the slaves, immediatists assumed a political position closer to that of the slaves. The desire to be "mere subjects" revealed that their identification with the plight of the slaves misguidedly translated into identification with the political position of the slaves. Thus, the understanding that slaves' "wrongs are my wrongs" transformed in the worst case into a belief that "their rights are my rights."[40] From a descriptive standpoint, this statement was not true. Northern abolitionists possessed the rights that slaves desired; they had the freedom that slaves sought. And as Frederick Douglass pointed out, these rights and freedoms meant that northern abolitionists had a moral responsibility toward effecting the slave's freedom as well as an inescapable obligation to enter the compromised and compromising world of politics.[41] Though he was well aware of the moral logic and persuasive force of the immediatist position, Douglass rightly refused to ignore its more devastating political and moral implications.

Revived Politics and Law

The immediatists' passionate moral conviction led to an unexpected result. They absented themselves from politics. Reluctant to compromise, they were unwilling to participate. They faced a dilemma similar to Socrates in the *Crito*. Should they obey unjust laws or should they flee in spirit from the polity that made those laws? Immediatists essentially chose to flee, not physically but internally to the realm of the conscience. As they saw it, democratic politics required citizens to dirty their hands. This they were unwilling to do.

Their unwillingness stemmed, in part, from their conception of democratic politics as a cohesive relationship between the people and government officials. Immediatists placed citizens and their representatives in a one-to-one, reciprocal relationship. Democratic citizens and their political representatives were united, for good or ill, and thus the acts of the latter reflected on the former. The significance of their political withdrawal

[39] Thoreau, *Higher Law*, 89–90.

[40] Ballou, "Address." Fanuzzi also points out that abolitionists like Thoreau and Douglass identified with slaves, and draws attention to beneficial aspects of this identification, noting that it challenged prevailing notions of citizenship and presented an alternative aesthetic of the public sphere. See "Thoreau's Civic Imagination" (167–203) and "Douglass's Sublime," (205–50) in Fanuzzi, *Abolition's Public Sphere*.

[41] Douglass, "Various Phases of Anti-Slavery."

becomes clear through a comparison with another faction of the movement that was equally hardheaded about the immorality of slavery. Radical political abolitionists were well aware of the view that politics was a "foul contamination"—indeed, many openly held this view—but they decided that the risk of taint was one that had to be taken. Rejecting the immediatists' escapism, the radicals turned back to institutional politics determined to change it as much as it might change them. Radical political abolitionists such as James Birney, Gerrit Smith, Samuel May, Frederick Douglass, and William Goodell could not understand how immediatist abolitionists could be "*in* the country, but at the same time . . . profess to stand outside of the Government," as Douglass put it.[42] Frustrated with the choice of presidential candidates in the 1844 election between the pro-slavery Whig, Henry Clay, and the Democrat, James K. Polk, they formed the Liberty Party and then the Liberty Party Abolitionists. And discouraged by the immediatist arguments for disunion, radicals argued that abolitionist goals were best served by staying both in the country and in the government.

In their endeavor the radical political abolitionists were assisted by the ideas, vigor, and passionate commitment to abolition of Lysander Spooner. It is important to note that the radical political abolitionists adopted Spooner; he did not adopt them. True to his individualistic anarchist principles and his steadfast faith in the irresistible power of natural law, Spooner was not a joiner. In fact, though he trained in law, Spooner never sought admission to the bar because he believed that its requirements discriminated against the well-educated poor. Spooner's characteristic response was to defy the rules. He became a lawyer without the bar by printing out cards that read, "Lysander Spooner, offers to the public his services in the Profession of the Law. Offices in the Central Exchange. Worcester, April 8, 1835." Also in characteristic fashion, he published a petition entitled "To the Members of the Legislature of Massachusetts" in the *Worcester Republican* criticizing the requirements to gain admission to the bar. These requirements were voted down by the Massachusetts legislature in 1836.[43]

Creatively co-opting Spooner, the radical political abolitionists were able to accept political complicity and to reconceptualize the relationship between citizens, the law, and political representation. They parted from the immediatists. Foremost, radicals rejected the notion that the meaning of constitutional law was fixed, and instead offered a fresh view of the document and urged a reassessment of the extent to which it protected slavery. Beginning with the fact the original document did not mention slavery or slaves, some radicals argued that the Constitution did not explicitly

[42] Foner, *Life and Writings of Frederick Douglass*, 5:366–71.
[43] Spooner, *Collected Works of Lysander Spooner*, 1:17–18.

support slavery. Still others argued that it was a thoroughly antislavery document.

In general, radicals made their case through three constitutional provisions.[44] First, they argued that the due process clause of the Fifth Amendment meant that no person in the United States could be deprived of his or her liberty without legally being declared a slave in a common-law proceeding and, as a consequence, that all individuals had a substantive right to liberty.[45] Second, radicals focused on the privileges and immunities clause. They argued that this clause protected each person who was born in the United States, or who pledged allegiance to the government, from incursions to basic rights, such as the right to marry, to own property, to move freely within the country, and to vote. Radicals expanded the definition of "citizen," in other words, so that slaves who were native born or who obligated themselves to the laws of their government would count as citizens.[46] Third, radicals interpreted the guarantee clause of Article IV, section 4, as meaning that every state was required to have a republican form of government that accorded to the ideals articulated in the Declaration of Independence.[47]

In short, radicals interpreted constitutional law in light of their values and morals, and interpretation was, in this respect, an act of autonomy and democracy. In some cases, these interpretations were strained, while in others, the radicals' daring worked insofar as it suggested a previously unforeseen constitutional world. Spooner, for instance, argued that the so-called slavery provisions of the Constitution did not mention slavery explicitly because they referred to resident aliens, not slaves. And in interpreting the three-fifths clause, Spooner argued that it applied to aliens, who, unlike full citizens, only partially benefited from the government's protection and only partially contributed to the strength and resources of the country. Thus, they should be *partially* counted as citizens—specifically, each counted as three-fifths of a citizen—for the purposes of taxation and representation. Spooner arrived at this interpretation through a steadfast commitment to the preeminence of higher law over positive law, a fanatical attention to the explicit words of the Constitution, and a thorough disregard for the intent of the framers or the historical record of the founding.[48]

[44] Many of the radical political abolitionists' ideas about what the Constitution should say were eventually adopted with the ratification of the Civil War Amendments. See TenBroek, *Antislavery Origins of the Fourteenth Amendment.*

[45] Stewart, "Constitutional Argument on the Subject of Slavery."

[46] Tiffany, *Treatise on the Unconstitutionality of American Slavery*; Yates, *Rights of Colored Men to Suffrage, Citizenship, and Trial by Jury.*

[47] Goodell, *Views of American Constitutional Law*; Parker, *Relation of Slavery to a Republican Form of Government.*

[48] Spooner, *Collected Works of Lysander Spooner*, 4:242–89, 155–236.

A virtue of the radicals' approach to the law was that it encouraged creativity and imagination. The rarity of the spirit of innovation is apparent in Emerson's critique of Daniel Webster, the secretary of state charged with enforcing the fugitive slave provision of the Constitution as well as the Fugitive Slave Act of 1850.[49] Denouncing Webster's formalist approach to law, Emerson described him as

> a man of the past, not a man of faith or hope. . . . He adheres to the letter. Happily, he was born late,—after the independence had been declared, the Union agreed to, and the Constitution settled. What he finds already written, he will defend. Lucky that so much had got well written when he came. For he has no faith in the power of self-government; none whatsoever in extemporizing a government. . . . In Massachusetts, in 1776, he would beyond all question have been a refugee. He praises Adams and Jefferson; but it is a past Adams and Jefferson that his mind can entertain. A present Adams and Jefferson he would denounce.[50]

Emerson's critique might have been leveled against the immediatists too. Both approached the law without a faith in self-government, as Emerson put it, and without a confidence in their capacity to create and improvise. If not wholly dead, the law was certainly moribund to them and they to it.[51]

Thoreau, in "Slavery in Massachusetts," makes a similar critique of legal formalism, though he infuses it with the metaphor of slavery:

> Do what you will, Oh Government! With my wife and children, my mother and brother, my father and my sister, and I will obey your commands to the letter. It will indeed grieve me if you hurt them, if you deliver them to the overseers to be hunted by hounds or to be whipped to death; but nevertheless, I will peaceably pursue my chosen calling on this fair earth, until perchance, one day, when I have put on mourning for them dead, I shall have persuaded you to relent.

Free citizens with an obsequious approach to government and a reverence for the law cease to be free. Thoreau urged an active and critical approach instead. Citizens should judge the law and legal officials, not only be judged by them. "Whoever has discerned truth has received his commis-

[49] On the rarity of the spirit of the Revolution, also see "The Revolutionary Tradition and Its Lost Treasure," in Arendt, *On Revolution*, 215–81.

[50] Emerson, *Emerson's Antislavery Writings*, 66–67.

[51] Spooner argued that citizens serving on juries have the right to judge both fact and law: "If a jury have not the right to judge between the government and those who disobey its laws, and resist its oppressions, the government is absolute, and the people *legally speaking* are slaves. Like many other slaves they may have sufficient courage to keep their masters somewhat in check; but they are nevertheless *known to the law* only as slaves." See the "Essay on Trial by Jury" in Spooner, *Collected Works of Lysander Spooner*, 2:1–11.

sion from a higher source than the chiefest justice in the world, who can discern only law. He finds himself constituted judge of the judge."[52]

At the same time however, radicals were largely unsuccessful at counterbalancing interpretation as autonomy from law with interpretation as domination by law. With the exception of Spooner, the radicals had the temperament to seek a position between democracy and constitutionalism. They founded the Liberty Party, for instance, which simultaneously declared independence from the established parties and submitted itself to the party structure in American politics. Yet the radicals were not able to fully articulate a complete approach to law that encompassed resistance and obligation, sovereignty and domination. And one is left to wonder what a constitutional interpretation that encompassed both of these elements might have looked like.

[52] Thoreau, *Higher Law*, 102 and 198.

Conclusion

A NATION OF PEOPLE OR LAWS

ON JANUARY 27, 1838, ABRAHAM LINCOLN delivered a moving and eloquent speech on one of the most pressing issues of his day: an outbreak of vigilante mobs in the South and North that were taking the law into their own hands and meting out punishment as they saw fit. The stakes of this kind of violence, Lincoln argued, were high. When mobs "spring up among the pleasure hunting masters of Southern slaves, and the order loving citizens in the land of steady habits," "this Government cannot last." As Lincoln saw it, the appearance of this "mobocratic spirit" raised the possibility of the nation's demise. "If destruction be our lot, we must ourselves be its author and finisher. As a nation of freemen, we must live through all time, or die by suicide."[1]

As Lincoln framed it, the citizenry faced a choice: If it wanted to be a thriving peaceful people, it could submit completely to the rule of law, or if it wanted to be a lawless, violent (and doomed) people, it could be governed by the rule of men. Lincoln contended the right choice was to embrace the law unquestioningly and to support political institutions wholeheartedly. Let reverence for the law, Lincoln argued, "become the *political religion* of the nation," and let all Americans "sacrifice unceasingly on its altars." Every citizen must remember "that to violate the law, is to trample on the blood of his father, and to tear the character of his own and his children's liberty."

Lincoln's forceful argument for the dominance of the rule of law is particularly worthy of reflection at the close of this book. A problem with Lincoln's either-or choice, it seems to me, is that it is an either-or choice. Lincoln's syllogism erases a third option—that is, that the tension between the rule of people and the rule of law be accepted rather than eradicated. In overlooking this alternative, Lincoln's prescription that the rule of law should always trump the rule of the people is problematic. The first casualty of such a move could be freedom and autonomy. The second could well be the rule of law.

[1] Basler, ed., *Collected Works*, 1:108–15. Unless otherwise noted, all Lincoln quotations are from the Lyceum Address.

Law as Political Religion

Lincoln's wholehearted embrace of the rule of law is certainly attractive. Before taking issue with his argument, it makes sense to briefly consider its appeal. Lincoln's idea of subjugation to the law has the virtue of taking the potential injustices of uncivil disobedience quite seriously. If we think primarily about the hapless and innocent victims of uncivil disobedience, then steadfast reverence for the law and unerring obedience to political institutions make a good deal of sense. Taking the perspective of the victim (or, more powerfully still, the perspective of a potential victim), the appeal of preserving innocent life, obeying political institutions, and respecting legal rights is tangible. As the Lyceum address makes clear, this was Lincoln's perspective. His thoughts were with the dead, those who were "seen literally dangling from the boughs of trees upon every road side; and in numbers almost sufficient, to rival the native Spanish moss of the country, as a drapery of the forest."

Lincoln's idea of subjugation to the law also makes intuitive sense because it reverses the dynamic between the rule of law and rule of people present in vigilantism and mob violence. While vigilantes and lynch mobs believed the rule of men should dominate the rule of law, Lincoln reverses this relationship and makes the rule of law preeminent. The corrective to mob violence, Lincoln argued, "is simple." "Let every American, every lover of liberty, every well wisher to his posterity, swear by the blood of the Revolution never to violate in the least particular, the laws of the country; and never to tolerate their violation by others." In place of the intemperate and wild demands of the mob, Lincoln urged his fellow Americans to embrace "reason, cold, calculating, unimpassioned reason . . . and, in particular, *a reverence for the constitution and laws*." And, as Lincoln saw it, veneration for the law should permeate numerous aspects of life. "Let reverence for the laws, be breathed by every American mother, to the lisping babe, that prattles in her lap—let it be taught in schools, in seminaries, and in colleges;—let it be written in Primmers, spelling books, and Almanacs;—let it be preached from the pulpit, proclaimed in legislative halls, and enforced in courts of justice." It is not hard to imagine how such complete admiration and awe for law might wholly displace the passionate, rowdy, and contemptuous spirit of uncivil disobedients.

Finally, Lincoln's notion of legal subjugation is appealing because he recognized that unjust laws exist and he acknowledged that some citizens will be vexed by obedience to them. Obedience to unjust laws is particularly onerous, he noted, when no legal provisions for redress exist. Whether redress was possible or not, Lincoln's counsel was the same: Citizens should wait for institutions to correct the law. Until institutions addressed the issue, unjust laws were still laws that required obedience. As long as these laws were valid, "they should be religiously observed." The time of revolutionary fervor, popular resistance, and passionate action, Lincoln argued, was past. The defiant scenes of the revolution "cannot be so universally known, nor so vividly felt, as they were by the generation just gone to rest." Rather than satisfying a desire to rule and attempting to relive the Revolution, citizens must support and maintain their political inheritance. Subjugation to the law may not be easy but, as Lincoln saw it, it was morally admirable and necessary for the preservation of American politics.

A difficulty with Lincoln's vision of complete and pure submission to the law is that it is oddly similar to the vigilante dream of unadulterated and absolute popular power. Taken at face value these two positions seem antithetical: Lincoln's normative vision implies the preeminence of laws, institutions, and procedures; the vigilante normative vision implies the preeminence of citizens, collective action, and ad hoc decision making. Yet both are visions of absolutism. Both seek to cancel the other out and are uncomfortable with the nagging questions and issues posed by the other. Vigilantes and lynch mobs had no patience for the law's plodding procedures or the opaque interworkings of legal institutions; their normative vision was one in which the people mastered the law, making it do their will.

In a similar way, Lincoln's Lyceum address seems equally ill at ease with popular and passionate demands for justice and seeks to contain them in omnipresent awe for the law. It too is drawn to oneness, homogeneity, and unity, though the binding factor is law, not popular will or morality. In this sense, the dream of absolute submission to the law and the ideal of absolute dominance over law are alike. Looked at from this vantage point, they seem more like two sides of the same coin rather than true opposites. The location of power certainly shifts radically between these two ideals. Still, the kind of power is similar, as is its intended effect of snuffing out disagreement and discord.

Reading Lincoln's eloquent and persuasive speech, I worry that the idealization of one form of absolute power—be it the absolute power of the law or the absolute power of the people—may invite its opposite. The desire for complete domination by the law may unexpectedly summon a desire for complete autonomy from law. Consider, for instance, that uncivil disobedients have initially felt dominated by law. Many accounts of uncivil disobedience are steeped in a sense of disempowerment and imbued with the bitterness of a grievance gone unheard. This phenomenon has begun with a sense of the unjust ascendancy of law and the estrangement from law. It begins where Lincoln ends, in other words: with submission and obedience to unjust law. But in the case of uncivil disobedience, submission to law has not engendered further submission, as Lincoln would have it. Rather, domination by law and alienation from government have given way to the desire to gratify a ruling passion and to dominate institutions and law.

As chapter 4 demonstrates, immediatist abolitionists experienced the domination of the law, and, much as Lincoln recommended, they pledged absolute obedience to the law, despite its injustices. Garrison and his compatriots, holding fast to their pacifism, could see no alternative but to pledge their allegiance to a Constitution they viewed as evil and unjust. Much as Lincoln urged, they endured bad laws and waited for institutions to act. Their decision did not result in institutional stability and peace, however. It resulted in the fugitive slave rescues and John Brown. In this case absolute domination by law fueled the dream of a complete escape from law and the ideal of pure autonomy and justice unfettered by institutions. As Lincoln suggested, this dynamic of absolute domination and absolute freedom has a powerful precursor in successful democratic revolutions. In victorious democratic revolutions, the experience of domination by unjust laws is followed by radical autonomy. Yet Lincoln's vision of complete submission to law may inadvertently regenerate this dynamic. His call to let go of all revolutionary fervor may counterintuitively re-animate it rather than putting it to rest.

It is important to note too that the idea of vacating popular power over law and institutions is a radical departure for American politics. The idea of taking power away from institutions and vesting it directly in the people has a long and venerated history in the United States. As James Morone has pointed out, it is the great American democratic wish.[2] Civil and uncivil disobedients are but two examples of a much broader tradition of appealing to the virtue of the people, the wisdom of the community, and the need to disseminate power to the citizenry. Consider, for instance, how Andrew Jackson's justification for rotation in office celebrates the common man: "The duties of all public officers are . . . so plain and simple that men of intelligence may readily qualify themselves for their performance."[3] Or, consider Lyndon Johnson's description of the War on Poverty as "a program which relies on the traditional time-tested American methods of organized local community action."[4] The American Revolutionaries proclaimed that the people were "out-of-doors," or outside of legal representative institutions, while almost two centuries

[2] Morone, *Democratic Wish*.
[3] Fish, *Civil Service and the Patronage*, 112.
[4] Sunquist, *On Fighting Poverty*, 23.

later Students for a Democratic Society declared, "democracy is in the streets."[5] As with uncivil disobedients, it is not entirely clear who exactly is a part of "the people" or a member of "the community," and these terms have a tendency to obscure diversity and difference within the community and among the people. Still, it is difficult to imagine American politics bereft of these terms, no matter how vague they can be or how often they distort the multiplicity of the citizenry.

Lawlessness

Lincoln's Lyceum address also gives pause if one imagines it being read by Rosa Parks, Martin Luther King Jr., or any of the countless citizens who violated the law during the civil rights movement. What if these citizens had sworn "never to violate in the least particular, the laws of the country; and never to tolerate their violation by others"? Or, one might rephrase this question in terms of Lincoln's own historical context. What if Lincoln had followed the advice he gave in the Lyceum address during the Civil War? It is likely that he would have conducted the war differently. As he noted in his 1864 letter to A. G. Hodges, the urgent circumstances of the Civil War demanded that "otherwise unconstitutional" measures be undertaken.

> Was it possible to lose the nation and yet preserve the Constitution? By general law, life and limb must be protected, yet often a limb must be amputated to save a life; but a life is never wisely given to save a limb. I felt that measures otherwise unconstitutional might become lawful by becoming indispensable to the preservation of the nation. Right or wrong, I assume this ground, and now avow it.[6]

In this frank account of his decision to value the preservation of the nation over the rule of law, Lincoln is some distance from celebrating the patriotic mother who instructs her prattling babe to venerate law. In contrast to the Lyceum address, he suggests that at some moments and in some circumstances, breaking the law may be the right thing to do.

Civil and uncivil disobedients remind us that the ground between lawlessness and lawfulness may be more difficult to discern than the Lyceum address allows for. As Lincoln presents it, one is either law abiding or law breaking; there is no middle ground. Yet in the distance between these two positions—between, say, the obedient citizen who scrupulously adheres to every law as a matter of sacred honor and the criminal who

[5] Wood, *Creation of the American Republic*, 319–28.

[6] Nicolay and Hay, *Complete Works of Abraham Lincoln*, 10:66.

breaks laws for his or her advantage—there is a fair amount of gray area. There are distinct kinds of law-breakers, and some of these lawless types may appear more legitimate than others because of their moral or political cause or because of the context in which they acted. Revolutionaries are not the same as vigilantes, who are not the thing as social bandits, exiles, or sovereigns wielding prerogative power in an emergency. It is important to note that the distinctions between these types are not just based on the intent of the lawbreakers. Rather, there are specific behaviors and arguments associated with various types of lawless action (vigilantes do not violate the law in the same way as revolutionaries or for the same reason). These actions and arguments contribute to how the law breaking is perceived by others and to their potential legitimacy. They shade the gray as it were.

What counts as breaking the law and why can be thorny questions. As mentioned in the introduction, scholars of vigilantism and lynching crowds have repeatedly emphasized the "lawless lawfulness" of this phenomenon, pointing out that these collective and public violations of the law were strangely enough understood as legitimate and lawful. Thus, vigilantes and lynch mobs have been described as "taking the law into their own hands," a phrase that suggests that vigilantes were doing something legal (though it is not clear *what*) at the same time as they were doing something illegal (ditto). To borrow from contemporary scholarship on law in a state of emergency or an exception, uncivil disobedients seem to be "inside" the law at the same time as they are clearly "outside" of it. In the Hodges letter, Lincoln himself gives insight into how complex the task of distinguishing between legal and illegal actions can be. He notes that his "otherwise unconstitutional" measures "might become lawful" because the results are beneficial. That is, they preserve the nation. Lawless actions could potentially flip and become lawful.

As I argued in chapter 3, the "lawless" side of uncivil disobedience is clarified by noting that lynch mobs in the post-Reconstruction South tended to suspend the law in specific, observable ways. Lynching crowds violated power-conferring rules. The same can be said of frontier vigilantes and of militant abolitionists who engaged in fugitive slave rescues. In this respect, these uncivil disobedients are distinct from disobedients in the civil rights movement who pointedly did not interfere with second-order rules that define how first-order rules (or duty-imposing rules) are authoritatively identified, changed, eliminated, or violated. Uncivil disobedients are closer to revolutionaries (though, as I have noted, not the same as revolutionaries) than disobedients in the civil rights movement were. Like revolutionaries, uncivil disobedients intervened in rules that governed legal officials, and they assumed the responsibilities of these officials. Unlike revolutionaries, however, their assumption of power was a temporary, stopgap measure and they typically had no interest in instigating a cataclysmic change in the political structure or in permanently assuming political power. Their actions were reformist not revolutionary.

The "lawful" or legitimate side of uncivil disobedience is more difficult to parse. Frontier vigilantes clearly mimicked legal authorities by conducting elaborate trials, and they readily used legal concepts, terms, and procedures in these proceedings. What's more, lawyers, judges, sheriffs, and legislators willingly joined vigilantes and heartily defended them. Much like participants in show trials however, vigilantes dispensed with the trappings of a trial when they interfered with their goals. And, like show trials, vigilante trials often were pro forma events in which everyone, including the victim, was well aware of how they would end. Vigilante acquittals were rare. Were frontier vigilantes really lawlike then? It is difficult to say. (And by this same measure, it is also difficult to say just how lawlike a criminal-justice system is in which plea bargaining is the norm. How lawlike is the law?)

Another aspect of legitimacy concerns results. Uncivil disobedients have gained legitimacy if the results of their actions are deemed beneficial. As Lincoln noted in the Hodges letter, consequences matter. So too does the amount of popular moral or political sympathy aroused by the group's grievances and goals. The legitimizing pull of widespread moral agreement is, in part, what makes violent abolitionism such an intriguing case. Government inaction can have a legitimizing effect as well. Lynching crowds in the South seemed more lawlike to the extent that local, regional, and national legal officials tolerated—and in some cases condoned—their lawlessness.

The question of the legitimacy of uncivil disobedients also brings one right back to the question of whether the people or the law ought to be supreme in liberal democracies. If constitutionalism should always trump democracy, then disobedients are always illegitimate. Civil or uncivil, sympathetic or not, and regardless of the political consequences, disobedience is lawless. Lincoln's position in the Lyceum address has the virtue of clarity and decisiveness. It vacates all the messy considerations of how an action that at first seems lawless might transform into something lawful or, more confusing still, quasi lawful. It also makes the "people" less ethereal and indistinct. The people are firmly housed in legal and political institutions; they are never out of doors.

Yet Lincoln's argument in the Lyceum address runs roughshod over what has become a persistent debate about the legitimacy of popular disobedience. Throughout American history, disobedience of all sorts has raised questions about the legitimacy of particular actions and, more generally, about the authority of a dissenting group to speak for the people. The scholarly debate about the legitimacy of lynch mobs and vigilantes reproduces this dispute at a different register but does not radically change it. The persistence of this argument is significant in itself. Popular disobedience has raised questions about legitimacy among a range of individuals (ordinary citizens, elites, scholars), within an array of media (broadsides, memoirs, manifestos, academic texts), and from the nineteenth to the twenty-first century. This suggests that the legitimacy or illegitimacy of popular disobedience is difficult to definitively determine. The debate about legitimacy nags because neither constitutionalism nor democracy has triumphed. This, it seems to me, is a good thing. To eliminate the tension between democracy and constitutionalism would deprive democratic politics of its full substance, rendering it a flat and scripted endeavor. To cut out the gray area between lawfulness and lawlessness would divest citizens of political discourse and judgment. If law is always already triumphant, then what is there to talk about or to judge?

In his Lyceum address Lincoln was right to worry about a populist ruling passion that profanes the rule of law and can result in cruel and arbitrary actions. By correcting one form of extremism with another, however, Lincoln endangers the spirit of autonomy. Utter submission to law might well encourage citizens to "live in the shadow of the other's presence, even if no arm is raised against them" and to find themselves in a position in which they are "unable to look the other in the eye," as Phillip Pettit has evocatively put it.[7] Democratic citizens who continually bend their heads in the shadow of law or who are unable to look those who embody the law in the eye have lost something vital to their citizenship. What's more, it is difficult to imagine that citizens worth the name would remain utterly submissive even to an ideal as vital as the rule of law. If the past is any guide, the impulse to reclaim autonomy will reappear, potentially in a more virulent and uncompromising form.

If, as I have suggested, the dream of absolute submission to the law is more problematic than it first appears and may fail to deliver on Lincoln's promise of peace and stability, then what is the alternative? How should the tension in liberal democracies between the rule of law and the rule of people be dispelled? Perhaps it shouldn't. Perhaps the goal of dissipating this tension is the wrong approach. An alternative is to accept it, understanding liberal democracies as positioned uncomfortably and precariously between these ideals. History suggests that there will likely be times when one ideal is more appealing than the other. Citizens in liberal democracies may well feel—and should feel—the allure of autonomy and the appeal of bringing the law to justice. To dream of complete autonomy from law, however, is a risky endeavor. There may be times when this type

[7] Pettit, *Republicanism*, 5.

of thinking and action is necessary. And it may not end badly. Still, history suggests it is hazardous.

Whatever the future holds, the past offers a final insight. Problems do not arise from disobedience alone, collective action itself, or a populist desire for autonomy and justice on its own. Instead, problems arise when disobedience is joined with the fantasy of eclipsing law completely and of eradicating its domination entirely. Disobedience is a risky endeavor, to be sure. But this fantasy makes it all the more so.

SOURCES CITED

Abanes, Richard. *American Militias: Rebellion, Racism and Religion*. Downers Grove, IL: InterVarsity Press, 1996.

Adamic, Louis. *Dynamite: The Story of Class Violence in America*. New York: Viking, 1934.

Allen, James. *Without Sanctuary: Lynching Photography in America*. Santa Fe, NM: Twin Palms, 2000.

Apter, David Ernest. *The Legitimization of Violence*. Basingstoke, UK: Macmillan Press 1997.

Arendt, Hannah. *On Revolution*. New York: Viking Press, 1965.

———. "On Violence." In *Crises of the Republic: Lying in Politics, Civil Disobedience on Violence, Thoughts on Politics, and Revolution*. New York: Harcourt Brace Jovanovich, 1972.

Aron, Stephen. *How the West Was Lost: The Transformation of Kentucky from Daniel Boone to Henry Clay*. Baltimore: Johns Hopkins University Press, 1996.

Ayers, Edward L. *The Promise of the New South: Life after Reconstruction*. New York: Oxford University Press, 1992.

———. *Vengeance and Justice: Crime and Punishment in the 19th Century American South*. New York: Oxford University Press, 1984.

Bakken, Gordon Morris. *Practicing Law in Frontier California*. Lincoln: University of Nebraska Press, 1991.

Bakunin, Mikhail Aleksandrovich. *The Political Philosophy of Bakunin: Scientific Anarchism*. Glencoe: Free Press, 1953.

Ballou, Adin. "Address." *Liberator*, September 22, 1842.

Bancroft, Hubert Howe. *The Works of Hubert Howe Bancroft*. 39 vols. San Francisco: History Company, 1887.

Barber, Benjamin R. *Strong Democracy: Participatory Politics for a New Age*. Berkeley: University of California Press, 1984.

Barkun, Michael. "Violence in the Name of Democracy: Justifications for Separatism on the Radical Right." In *The Democratic Experience and Political Violence*, edited by David C. Rapoport and Leonard Weinberg, 193–208. London: F. Cass, 2001.

Barnes, Gilbert Hobbs. *The Antislavery Impulse, 1830–1844*. New York: Harcourt Brace and World, 1964.

Basler, Roy P., ed. *The Collected Works of Abraham Lincoln*. 9 vols. New Brunswick, NJ: Rutgers University Press, 1959.

Beck, E. M., and Stewart Emory Tolnay. "When Race Didn't Matter: Black and White Mob Violence against Their Own Color." In *Under Sentence of Death: Lynching in the South*, edited by W. Fitzhugh Brundage, 132–54. Chapel Hill: University of North Carolina Press, 1997.

Berlet, Chip, and Matthew Lyons. *Right-Wing Populism in America: Too Close for Comfort*. New York: Guilford Press, 2000.
Bickel, Alexander M. *The Least Dangerous Branch: The Supreme Court at the Bar of Politics*. 2nd ed. Indianapolis, IN: Bobbs-Merrill, 1962.
Birney, James Gillespie, and William Lloyd Garrison. *A Letter on the Political Obligations of Abolitionists, The Anti-Slavery Crusade in America*. New York: Arno Press, 1969.
Bodenhamer, David J., and James W. Ely. *Ambivalent Legacy: A Legal History of the South*. Jackson: University Press of Mississippi, 1984.
Bonaparte, Charles J. "Lynch Law and Its Remedy." *Yale Law Journal* 8, no. 8 (1899): 335–43.
Bork, Robert. "Neutral Principles and Some First Amendment Problems." In *Interpreting the Constitution: The Debate over Original Intent*, edited by Jack N. Rakove, 197–226. Boston: Northeastern University Press, 1990.
Bosmajian, Haig A., and Hamida Bosmajian. *The Rhetoric of the Civil-Rights Movement*. New York: Random House, 1969.
Branch, Taylor. *Parting the Waters: America in the King Years, 1954–1963*. New York: Simon and Schuster, 1988.
Breitman, George, ed. *Malcolm X Speaks*. New York: Grove Press, 1965.
Brewer, Charles B. "Some Follies in Our Criminal Procedure." *McClure's Magazine* 34, no. 6 (1910): 677–86.
Brewer, David J. "The Right of Appeal." *Independent* (1903): 2547–50.
Brown, Richard Maxwell. *Strain of Violence: Historical Studies of American Violence and Vigilantism*. New York: Oxford University Press, 1975.
Brown, Wendy. "Guns, Cowboys, Philadelphia Mayors and Civic Republicanism: On Sanford Levinson's the Embarrassing Second Amendment." *Yale Law Journal* 99, no. 3 (1989): 661.
Browne, John W. "Speech at the Anniversary of the New York Young Men's Anti-Slavery Society." *Liberator*, June 23, 1837.
Brundage, W. Fitzhugh. *Lynching in the New South: Georgia and Virginia, 1880–1930*. Urbana: University of Illinois Press, 1993.
Carson, Clayborne, ed. *The Movement: 1964–1970*. Westport, CT: Greenwood Press, 1993.
Caughey, John Walton. *Their Majesties, the Mob*. Chicago: University of Chicago Press, 1960.
Chadbourn, James Harmon. *Lynching and the Law*. Chapel Hill: University of North Carolina Press, 1933.
Chambers, Simone, and Jeffrey Kopstein. "Bad Civil Society." *Political Theory* 29, no. 6 (2001): 837–65.
Chan, Sucheng. "A People of Exceptional Character: Ethnic Diversity, Nativism, and Racism in the California Gold Rush " In *Rooted in Barbarous Soil: People, Culture, and Community in Gold Rush California*, edited by Kevin Starr and Richard J. Orsi, 44–85. Berkeley: University of California Press, 2000.
Child, Lydia Maria Francis. *An Appeal in Favor of That Class of Americans Called Africans*. Boston: Allen and Ticknor, 1833.
Clark, Walter. "The True Remedy for Lynch Law." *American Law Review* 28, no. November–December (1894): 800–807.

"A Clerical Editor's Opinion." *New York Times*, April 24, 1899.

The Colonizationist and Journal of Freedom. April 1833–April 1834 vol. Boston: Geo. W. Light, 1834.

Congressional Record, 56th Congress, First Session, February 1, 1900.

"Constitutionality of Slavery." *Massachusetts Quarterly Review* 4 (1848): 463–509.

Cover, Robert M. *Justice Accused: Antislavery and the Judicial Process*. New Haven: Yale University Press, 1975.

Cozic, Charles P. *The Militia Movement*. San Diego: Greenhaven Press, 1997.

Cutler, James Elbert. *Lynch-Law: An Investigation into the History of Lynching in the United States*. New York: Negro University Press, 1969.

Dane, G. Ezra, and Beatrice J. Dane. *Ghost Town, Wherein Is Told Much That Is Wonderful, Laughable, and Tragic, and Some That Is Hard to Believe, About Life During the Gold Rush and Later in the Town of Columbia on California's Mother Lode, as Remembered by the Oldest Inhabitants and Here for the First Time Set Down by G. Ezra Dane, in Collaboration with Beatrice J. Dane*. 1st ed. New York: A. A. Knopf, 1941.

Davis, David Brion. *The Problem of Slavery in the Age of Revolution, 1770–1823*. Ithaca, NY: Cornell University Press, 1975.

———. *The Problem of Slavery in Western Culture*. Ithaca, NY: Cornell University Press, 1969.

Dees, Morris, and James Corcoran. *Gathering Storm: America's Militia Threat*. New York: HarperCollins Publishers, 1996.

Dimsdale, Thomas J. *The Vigilantes of Montana; or, Popular Justice in the Rocky Mountains. Being a Correct and Impartial Narrative of the Chase, Trial, Capture, and Execution of Henry Plummer's Road Agent Band, Together with Accounts of the Lives and Crimes of Many of the Robbers and Desperadoes, the Whole Being Interspersed with Sketches of Life in the Mining Camps of the "Far West."* Rev. ed. Norman: University of Oklahoma Press, 1953.

Douglass, Frederick. "The Various Phases of Anti-Slavery." *Frederick Douglass' Paper*, November 16, 1855.

Dray, Philip. *At the Hands of Persons Unknown: The Lynching of Black America*. New York: Random House, 2002.

Dumond, Dwight Lowell. *Antislavery: The Crusade for Freedom in America*. Ann Arbor: University of Michigan Press, 1961.

Dyer, Joel. *Harvest of Rage: Why Oklahoma City Is Only the Beginning*. Boulder, CO: Westview Press, 1997.

Elkins, Stanley M. *Slavery: A Problem in American Institutional and Intellectual Life*. 2nd ed. Chicago: University of Chicago Press, 1968.

Ellis, Richard J. *The Dark Side of the Left: Illiberal Egalitarianism in America*. Lawrence: University Press of Kansas, 1998.

Elster, Jon, and Rune Slagstad, eds. *Constitutionalism and Democracy*. New York: Cambridge University Press, 1988.

Emerson, Ralph Waldo. *Emerson's Antislavery Writings*. New Haven: Yale University Press, 1995.

Ex Parte Wall, 107 U.S. 265 (1883).

"Excitement at Palmetto." *Atlanta Constitution*, April 15, 1899.

Fanon, Frantz. *The Wretched of the Earth*. Translated by Constance Farrington. New York: Grove Press, 1963.

Fanuzzi, Robert. *Abolition's Public Sphere*. Minneapolis: University of Minnesota Press, 2003.

Faragher, John Mack. *Women and Men on the Overland Trail*. New Haven: Yale University Press, 1979.

"Fiendish Negro Lynched in Bossier." *Daily Picayune, New Orleans*, November 3, 1903.

Filler, Louis. *The Crusade against Slavery, 1830–1860*. New York: Harper and Row, 1960.

Fish, Carl Russell. *The Civil Service and the Patronage*. New York: Russell and Russell, 1963.

Foner, Philip S., ed. *The Life and Writings of Frederick Douglas*, (New York: International Publishers, 1950).

———. *We, the Other People: Alternative Declarations of Independence by Labor Groups, Farmers, Woman's Rights Advocates, Socialists, and Blacks, 1829–1975*. Urbana: University of Illinois Press, 1976.

Forman, James. *The Making of Black Revolutionaries*. 2nd ed. Washington, DC: Open Hand Pub., 1985.

Friedman, Lawrence M. *A History of American Law*. 3rd ed. New York: Simon and Schuster, 2005.

Friedman, Leon. *The Wise Minority*. New York: Dial Press, 1971.

Friends, Society of. *Germantown Friends' Protest against Slavery, 1688*. Germantown, PA, 1688.

"Gerrit Smith's Constitutional Argument No. III." *Liberator*, October 4, 1844.

Ginzburg, Ralph. *100 Years of Lynchings*. Baltimore: Black Classic Press, 1988.

Goodell, William. *Views of American Constitutional Law in Its Bearing upon American Slavery*. 2nd ed, *Black Heritage Library Collection*. Freeport, NY: Books for Libraries Press, 1971.

Gordon, Linda. *The Great Arizona Orphan Abduction*. Cambridge, MA: Harvard University Press, 1999.

"Governor Blames the Negroes." *New York Times*, April 24, 1899.

Graham, Hugh Davis, and Ted Robert Gurr, eds. *Violence in America: Historical and Comparative Perspectives*. 2 vols. Newbury Park: Sage Publications, 1969.

Griffin, Larry J., Paula Clark, and Joanne C. Sandberg. "Narrative and Event: Lynching and Historical Sociology." In *Under Sentence of Death: Lynching in the South*, edited by W. Fitzhugh Brundage. Chapel Hill: University of North Carolina Press, 1997.

Grimsted, David. *American Mobbing, 1828–1861*. New York: Oxford University Press, 1998.

"Guardsmen Put Condemned Trio Back into Cells." *Jackson Daily Clarion Ledger*, February 13, 1934.

Habermas, J. "Constitutional Democracy—a Paradoxical Union of Contradictory Principles?" *Political Theory* 29, no. 6 (2001): 766–81.

Hacker, P.M.S., and Joseph Raz. *Law, Morality, and Society: Essays in Honour of H.L.A. Hart*. Oxford: Clarendon Press, 1977.

Hailey, Foster. "Birmingham Talks Pushed; Negroes March Peacefully." *New York Times* May 6, 1963.
Hall, Jacquelyn Dowd. *Revolt against Chivalry: Jessie Daniel Ames and the Women's Campaign against Lynching*. Rev. ed. New York: Columbia University Press, 1993.
Hamilton, Neil A. *Militias in America: A Reference Handbook*. Santa Barbara, CA: Abc-Clio, 1996.
Hamilton, William Baskerville. *Anglo-American Law of the Frontier: Thomas Rodney and His Territorial Cases*. Durham: Duke University Press, 1953.
Hart, H.L.A. *The Concept of Law*. Oxford: Clarendon Press, 1961.
Hartz, Louis. *The Liberal Tradition in America: An Interpretation of American Political Thought since the Revolution*. 2nd Harvest/HBJ ed. San Diego, CA: Harcourt Brace Jovanovich, 1991.
"He Cannot Escape, They Say." *Atlanta Constitution*, April 18, 1899.
Hine, Robert V. *The American West: An Interpretive History*. Boston: Little Brown, 1973.
Hobbes, Thomas. *Leviathan*. Edited by Richard Tuck. Cambridge, UK: Cambridge University Press, 1996.
Hofstadter, Richard, and Michael Wallace. *American Violence: a Documentary History*. 1st ed. New York: Knopf, 1970.
Holland, Catherine A. *The Body Politic: Foundings, Citizenship, and Difference in the American Political Imagination*. New York: Routledge, 2001.
Holmes, Stephen. *Passions and Constraint: On the Theory of Liberal Democracy*. Chicago: University of Chicago Press, 1995.
Honig, Bonnie. "Between Decision and Deliberation: Political Paradox in Democratic Theory." *American Political Science Review* 101, no. 1 (2007): 1–17.
———. "Dead Rights, Live Futures: A Reply to Habermas's 'Constitutional Democracy.'" *Political Theory* 29, no. 6 (2001): 792.
"Hose Is a Will 'O the Wisp to His Determined Pursuers." *Atlanta Constitution*, April 16, 1899.
Hurtado, Albert L. *Intimate Frontiers: Sex, Gender, and Culture in Old California*. Albuquerque: University of New Mexico Press, 1999.
In Re Wall, 13 F. 814 (1882).
Ingalls, Robert P. "Lynching and Establishment Violence in Tampa, 1858–1935." *Journal of Southern History* 53, no. 4 (1987): 613–44.
———. *Urban Vigilantes in the New South: Tampa, 1882–1936*. Knoxville: University of Tennessee Press, 1988.
Inverarity, James M. . "Populism and Lynching in Louisiana." In *Lynching, Racial Violence, and the Law*, edited by Paul Finkelman, 208–26. New York: Garland Publishing, 1992.
Johnson, David A. "Vigilance and the Law: The Moral Authority of Popular Justice in the Far West." *American Quarterly* 33, no. 5, Special Issue: American Culture and the American Frontier (1981): 558–86.
Johnson, Susan Lee. *Roaring Camp: The Social World of the California Gold Rush*. New York: W.W. Norton, 2000.
Johnston, Steven. *Encountering Tragedy: Rousseau and the Project of Democratic Order*. Ithaca, NY: Cornell University Press, 1999.

"Judge Locke V. General Wall." *Tampa Sunland Tribune*, March 16, 1882.

Juergensmeyer, Mark. *Terror in the Mind of God: The Global Rise of Religious Violence*. Berkeley: University of California Press, 2003.

Kaminski, John P., and Richard Leffler, eds. *Federalists and Antifederalists: The Debate over the Ratification of the Constitution*. Vol 1. Madison, WI: Madison House, 1998.

Kateb, George. "Wolin as a Critic of Democracy." In *Democracy and Vision: Sheldon Wolin and the Vicissitudes of the Political*, edited by Aryeh Botwinick and William E. Connolly, 39–57. Princeton: Princeton University Press, 2001.

Kaufman-Osborn, Timothy V. *From Noose to Needle: Capital Punishment and the Late Liberal State*. Ann Arbor: University of Michigan, 2002.

Kendall, John S. "Who Killa De Chief?" *Louisiana Historical Quarterly* 22 (1939): 492–530.

King, Clarence. *Mountaineering in the Sierra Nevada*. Edited by Francis Peloubet Farquhar. Lincoln: University of Nebraska Press, 1997.

King, Martin Luther, Jr. *Why We Can't Wait*. New York: Signet Books, 1964.

Klarman, Michael J. *From Jim Crow to Civil Rights: The Supreme Court and the Struggle for Racial Equality*. Oxford, UK: Oxford University Press, 2004.

Kraditor, Aileen S. *Means and Ends in American Abolitionism: Garrison and His Critics on Strategy and Tactics, 1834–1850*. New York: Pantheon Books, 1969.

Kramer, Larry. *The People Themselves: Popular Constitutionalism and Judicial Review* Oxford, UK: Oxford University Press, 2004.

Kunstler, William Moses. *Deep in My Heart*. New York: Morrow, 1966.

Lakey, George. *Strategy for a Living Revolution*. New York: Grossman Publishers, 1973.

Lamar, Howard Roberts. *The New Encyclopedia of the American West*. New Haven: Yale University Press, 1998.

Lane, Roger. *Murder in America: A History*. Columbus: Ohio State University Press, 1997.

Lang, H. O. *A History of Tuolumne County, California*. San Francisco: B. F. Alley, 1882.

Langum, David J. *Law and Community on the Mexican California Frontier: Anglo-American Expatriates and the Clash of Legal Traditions, 1821–1846*. Norman: University of Oklahoma Press, 1987.

Laue, James H. *Direct Action and Desegregation, 1960–1962: Toward a Theory of the Rationalization of Protest*. Brooklyn: Carlson Publishing, 1989.

LaVaque-Manty, Mika. *Arguments and Fists: Political Agency and Justification in Liberal Theory*. New York: Routledge, 2002.

Levy, JoAnn. *They Saw the Elephant: Women in the California Gold Rush*. Norman: University of Oklahoma Press, 1992.

Levy, Peter B. *Documentary History of the Modern Civil Rights Movement*. New York: Greenwood Press, 1992.

Lewis, H. T., Lewis W. Thomas, John C. McDonald, G. P. Munro, W. C. Glenn, and Burton Smith. "Is Lynch Law Due to Defects in the Criminal Law, or Its Administration?" Paper presented at the Fourteenth Annual Session of the Georgia Bar Association 1897.

"Liberty Party Defined." *Liberator*, November 11, 1842.

Limerick, Patricia Nelson. *Something in the Soil: Legacies and Reckonings in the New West*. 1st ed. New York: W.W. Norton, 2000.
Locke, John. *Two Treatises of Government*. Edited by Peter Laslett. Cambridge: Cambridge University Press, 1988.
"Lynching of a Ravisher-Murderer in Bienville." *New Orleans Picayune*, May 24, 1881.
Lynd, Staughton. *Intellectual Origins of American Radicalism*. New York: Vintage Books, 1969.
MacCormick, Neil. *H.L.A. Hart*. London: Arnold, 1981.
MacLean, Nancy. *Behind the Mask of Chivalry: The Making of the Second Ku Klux Klan*. New York: Oxford University Press, 1994.
———. "Gender, Sexuality, and the Politics of Lynching." In *Under Sentence of Death: Lynching in the South*, edited by W. Fitzhugh Brundage, 158–88. Chapel Hill: University of North Carolina Press, 1997.
———. "The Leo Frank Case Reconsidered: Gender and Sexual Politics in the Making of Reactionary Populism." *The Journal of American History* 78, no. 3 (1991): 917–48.
"A Man Hanged in Tampa." *Tampa Sunland Tribune*, March 9, 1882.
"Marchers Go Undoused in Sunday Demonstration." *Birmingham World*, May 8, 1963.
Marx, Karl. *Capital, a Critique of Political Economy*. New York: Modern library, 1936.
Marx, Karl, and Friedrich Engels. *Karl Marx, Frederick Engels: Collected Works*. Translated by Richard Dixon. 50 vols. London: Lawrence and Wishart, 1975.
McGovern, James R. *Anatomy of a Lynching: The Killing of Claude Neal*. Baton Rouge: Louisiana State University Press, 1982.
McKivigan, John R., and Stanley Harold. *Antislavery Violence: Sectional, Racial, and Cultural Conflict in Antebellum America*. 1st ed. Knoxville: University of Tennessee Press, 1999.
McPherson, James M. *The Abolitionist Legacy: From Reconstruction to the NAACP*. Princeton: Princeton University Press, 1975.
Meese, Edwin. "Interpreting the Constitution." In *Interpreting the Constitution: The Debate over Original Intent*, edited by Jack N. Rakove, 13–21. Boston: Northeastern University Press, 1990.
Miller, Joshua. "The Ghostly Body Politic: The Federalist Papers and Popular Sovereignty." *Political Theory* 16, no. 1 (1988): 99–119.
Miller v. Texas, 153 U.S. 535 (1894).
"Mississippi: Father's Right to Kill Approved by Senate." *Newsweek*, March 17, 1934.
"Mob after Hose: Be Lynched If Caught." *Atlanta Constitution*, April 14, 1899.
Morone, James A. *The Democratic Wish: Popular Participation and the Limits of American Government*. New York: Basic Books, 1990.
———. *Hellfire Nation: The Politics of Sin in American History*. New Haven: Yale University Press, 2003.
Mott, M. H. *History of the Regulators of Northern Indiana. Published by Order of the Central Committee*. Indianapolis: Indianapolis Journal Company Printers, 1859.

"Mrs. Alfred Cranford Talks." *Salt Lake City Broad Ax*, June 6, 1899, 1899.

"A Murder and Lynching in Concordia Parish." *New Orleans Picayune*, September 14, 1894.

Murphy, Jeffrie G., ed. *Civil Disobedience and Violence*. Belmont, MA: Wadsworth 1971.

"Negro Burned at a Tree." *New York Daily Tribune*, April 24, 1899.

"A Negro Murderer Slain by Indignant Negroes." *New Orleans Picayune*, June 27, 1890.

Newman, Richard S. *The Transformation of American Abolitionism: Fighting Slavery in the Early Republic*. Chapel Hill: University of North Carolina Press, 2002.

Nicolay, John G., and John Hay, eds. *Complete Works of Abraham Lincoln*. 12 vols. New York: F. D. Tandy Company, 1905.

Nudelman, Franny. *John Brown's Body: Slavery, Violence, and the Culture of War, Cultural Studies of the United States*. Chapel Hill; London: University of North Carolina Press, 2004.

Otis, James. *Some Political Writings of James Otis, the University of Missouri Studies, Vol. IV, Nos. 3 and 4*. Columbia: University of Missouri, 1929.

Paley, William. *The Principles of Moral and Political Philosophy*. 12th ed. London: R. Faulder, 1799.

Parker, Theodore. *The Relation of Slavery to a Republican Form of Government. A Speech Delivered at the New England Anti-Slavery Convention, Wednesday Morning, May 26, 1858*. Boston: W. L. Kent and Co., 1858.

Paul, Rodman W., and Elliott West. *Mining Frontiers of the Far West, 1848–1880*. Rev. and expanded ed. *Histories of the American Frontier*. Albuquerque: University of New Mexico Press, 2001.

Pennsylvania Society for Promoting the Abolition of Slavery. *The Constitution of the Pennsylvania Society, for Promoting the Abolition of Slavery, and the Relief of Free Negroes, Unlawfully Held in Bondage*. Philadelphia: F. Bailey, 1788.

Perry, Lewis. *Radical Abolitionism: Anarchy and the Government of God in Antislavery Thought*. Knoxville: University of Tennessee Press, 1995.

Pettit, Philip. *Republicanism: A Theory of Freedom and Government*. Oxford: Oxford University Press, 1997.

Pfeifer, Michael J. *Rough Justice: Lynching and American Society, 1874–1947*. Urbana: University of Illinois Press, 2004.

Phillips, Charles, and Alan Axelrod. *Encyclopedia of the American West*. New York: Simon and Schuster Macmillan, 1996.

Phillips, Wendell. *The Constitution a Pro-Slavery Compact: Or, Selections from the Madison Papers, Etc*. New York: American Antislavery Society, 1845.

———. "No-Voting Theory." *Liberator*, July 26, 1844.

———. *Review of Lysander Spooner's Essay on the Unconstitutionality of Slavery. Reprinted from The "Anti-Slavery Standard," with Additions*. Boston: Andrews and Prentiss, 1847.

"Posse Went out to Look at Him." *Atlanta Constitution*, April 22, 1899.

Pound, Roscoe. "The Causes of Popular Dissatisfaction with the Administration of Justice." In *The Pound Conference: Perspectives on Justice in the Future*, 337–53. St. Paul, MN: West Publishing Company, 1976.

Prassel, Frank Richard. *The Western Peace Officer: A Legacy of Law and Order*. Norman: University of Oklahoma Press, 1972.

Presser v. Illinois, 116 U.S. 252 (1886).

"Prisoners Move from Hinds Jail with Big Escort." *Jackson Daily Clarion Ledger*, February 12, 1934.

"Progress of the Anti-Slavery Movement." *Liberator*, January 28, 1842.

"Prospectus of the Liberator, Volume viii." *Liberator*, December 15, 1837.

Rable, George C. "The South and the Politics of Antilynching Legislation, 1920–1940." *Journal of Southern History*, vol. 51, no. 2 (May 1985): 201–20.

Rakove, Jack N. *Original Meanings: Politics and Ideas in the Making of the Constitution*. New York: A. A. Knopf, 1996.

Raper, Arthur F. *The Tragedy of Lynching*. Montclair, NJ: Patterson Smith, 1969.

Rapoport, David C., and Leonard Weinberg, eds. *The Democratic Experience and Political Violence*. London: F. Cass, 2001.

Reid, John Phillip. *Law for the Elephant: Property and Social Behavior on the Overland Trail*. San Marino, CA: Huntington Library, 1997.

———. *Policing the Elephant: Crime, Punishment, and Social Behavior on the Overland Trail*. San Marino, CA: Huntington Library, 1997.

Reynolds, David S. *John Brown, Abolitionist: The Man Who Killed Slavery, Sparked the Civil War, and Seeded Civil Rights*. 1st ed. New York: Alfred A. Knopf, 2005.

Ridge, Martin. "Disorder, Crime, and Punishment in the California Gold Rush." *Montana: The Magazine of Western History* 49, no. 3 (1999): 11–27.

Rohrbough, Malcolm. "No Boy's Play: Migration and Settlement in Early Gold Rush California." In *Rooted in Barbarous Soil: People, Culture, and Community in Gold Rush California*, edited by Kevin Starr and Richard J. Orsi, 25–43. Berkeley: University of California Press, 2000.

Rosenbaum, H. Jon, and Peter C. Sederberg. *Vigilante Politics*. Philadelphia: University of Pennsylvania Press, 1976.

Rosenblum, Nancy. *Membership and Morals: The Personal Uses of Pluralism in America*. Princeton: Princeton University Press, 1998.

Rousseau, Jean-Jacques. *On the Social Contract with Geneva Manuscript and Political Economy*. Translated by Judith R. Masters. Edited by Roger D. Masters. New York: St. Martin's, 1978.

Royce, Josiah. *California, from the Conquest in 1846 to the Second Vigilance Committee in San Francisco: a Study of American Character*. Boston: Houghton Mifflin and Company, 1886.

"Sam Holt Believed to Be Near Scene of His Crime." *Atlanta Constitution*, April 21, 1899.

"Sam Holt Now Believed to Have Been Located near Cusseta, Ala." *Atlanta Constitution*, April 23, 1899.

"Sam Holt, Murderer and Assailant, Burned at the Stake at Newnan." *Atlanta Constitution*, April 24, 1899.

San Francisco Vigilance Committee of '56, with Some Interesting Sketches of Events Succeeding 1846. San Francisco, CA: Barry Baird and Co., 1883.

Sarat, Austin. "Capital Punishment as Legal, Political, and Cultural Fact: An Introduction." In *The Killing State: Capital Punishment in Law, Politics, and*

Culture, edited by Austin Sarat, xi, 5, 263. New York: Oxford University Press, 1999.

Sartre, Jean-Paul. "Preface." To *The Wretched of the Earth*. New York: Grove Press, 1963.

Saxonhouse, Arlene W. *Fear of Diversity: The Birth of Political Science in Ancient Greek Thought*. Chicago: University of Chicago Press, 1992.

Schmitt, Carl. *The Crisis of Parliamentary Democracy*. Translated by Ellen Kennedy. Cambridge, MA: MIT Press, 1985.

Sewell, Richard H. *Ballots for Freedom: Antislavery Politics in the United States, 1837–1860*. New York: Oxford University Press, 1976.

"Shame to Mississippi." *The Nation*, January 16, 1929.

Shanks, Caroline L. "The Biblical Anti-Slavery Argument of the Decade, 1830–1840." *Journal of Negro History* 16, no. 2 (1931): 132–57.

Shapiro, Herbert. *White Violence and Black Response: From Reconstruction to Montgomery*. Amherst: University of Massachusetts Press, 1988.

Shinn, Charles Howard. *Mining Camps: A Study in American Frontier Government*. New York: C. Scribner's Sons, 1885.

Shklar, Judith N. *Men and Citizens: A Study of Rousseau's Social Theory*. London: Cambridge University Press, 1969.

Slotkin, Richard. *Regeneration through Violence: The Mythology of the American Frontier, 1600–1860*. Middletown, CT: Wesleyan University Press, 1974.

Smith, Kimberly K. *Dominion of Voice: Riot, Reason, and Romance in Antebellum Politics*. Lawrence: University Press of Kansas, 1999.

Smith, Rogers. *Civic Ideals: Conflicting Visions of Citizenship in U.S. History*. New Haven: Yale University Press, 1997.

Snyder, R. Claire. *Citizen-Soldiers and Manly Warriors: Military Service and Gender in the Civic Republican Tradition*. Lanham, MD: Rowman and Littlefield Publishers, 1999.

Sorel, Georges. *Reflections on Violence*. Translated by T.E. Hulme and J. Roth. Glencoe, IL: Free Press, 1950.

Spooner, Lysander. *The Collected Works of Lysander Spooner*. 6 vols. Weston, MA: M and S Press, 1971.

Stevens, Charles Emery. *Anthony Burns, a History*. Boston: J. P. Jewett and Company, 1856.

Stewart, Alvan. "A Constitutional Argument on the Subject of Slavery." In *Equality under Law*, edited by Jacobus tenBroeck, appendix B, pp. 281–95. New York: Collier Books, 1837.

Subcommittee of the Committee on the Judiciary. *Punishment for the Crime of Lynching; Hearings before a Subcommittee of the Committee on the Judiciary, United States Senate, Seventy-Third Congress, Second Session, on S. 1978, a Bill to Assure to Persons within the Jurisdiction of Every State the Equal Protection of the Laws and to Punish the Crime of Lynching*. February 20 and 21, 1934.

———. *To Prevent and Punish the Crime of Lynching. Hearing, Sixty-Ninth Congress, First Session, on S. 121*, February 16, 1926.

Sunquist, James L., ed. *On Fighting Poverty: Perspectives from Experience*. New York: American Academy of Arts and Sciences, 1969.

"Supreme Court Openly Defied in Chattanooga." *Birmingham Age–Herald*, March 20, 1904.

Sydnor, Charles S. "The Southerner and the Laws." *Journal of Southern History* 6, no. 1 (1940): 3–23.

Taylor, Quintard. "African American Men in the American West, 1528–1990." *American Academy of Political and Social Science* 569, no. 102 (2000): 103–16.

TenBroek, Jacobus. *The Antislavery Origins of the Fourteenth Amendment*. Berkeley: University of California Press, 1951.

Thomas, John L. *The Liberator, William Lloyd Garrison: A Biography*. 1st ed. Boston: Little Brown, 1963.

Thomas, Maurice. "The Court of Judge Lynch." *Lippencott's Monthly Magazine* 64, no. 380 (1899): 254–62.

Thoreau, Henry David. *The Higher Law: Thoreau of Civil Disobedience and Reform*. Princeton: Princeton University Press, 2004.

"Three Negroes Doomed; Troops Check Mob." *New York Times*, February 13, 1934.

Tiffany, Joel. *A Treatise on the Unconstitutionality of American Slavery, Together with the Powers and Duties of the Federal Government in Relation to That Subject*. Miami, FL: Mnemosyne Pub. Co., 1969.

Tocqueville, Alexis de. *Democracy in America*. Translated by Arthur Goldhammer. New York: Library of America 2004.

Tolnay, Stewart Emory, and E. M. Beck. *A Festival of Violence: An Analysis of Southern Lynchings, 1882–1930*. Urbana: University of Illinois Press, 1995.

Tracy, James. *Direct Action: Radical Pacifism from the Union Eight to the Chicago Seven*. Chicago: University of Chicago Press, 1996.

Urbinati, Nadia. *Representative Democracy: Principles and Genealogy*. Chicago: University of Chicago Press, 2006.

U.S. v. Cruikshank, 92 U.S. 542 (1876).

U.S. v. Miller, 307 U.S. 174 (1939).

Von Frank, Albert J. *The Trials of Anthony Burns: Freedom and Slavery in Emerson's Boston*. Cambridge: Harvard University Press, 1998.

Waldrep, Christopher. *The Many Faces of Judge Lynch: Extralegal Violence and Punishment in America*. New York: Palgrave Macmillan, 2002.

———. "War of Words: The Controversy over the Definition of Lynching, 1899–1940." *Journal of Southern History* 66, no. 1 (2000): 75–100.

Waldron, Jeremy. *Law and Disagreement*. New York: Oxford University Press, 2001.

———. "Precommitment and Disagreement." In *Constitutionalism: Philosophical Foundations*, edited by Larry Alexander, 271–99. Cambridge, UK: Cambridge University Press, 1998.

Walzer, Michael. *Just and Unjust Wars: A Moral Argument with Historical Illustrations*. New York: Basic Books, 1977.

———. *Obligations: Essays on Disobedience, War, and Citizenship*. Cambridge, MA: Harvard University Press, 1970.

———. "Political Action: The Problem of Dirty Hands." *Philosophy and Public Affairs* 2, no. 2 (1973): 160–80.

Weber, Max. *Weber: Political Writings*. Cambridge, UK: Cambridge University Press, 1994.

Wells-Barnett, Ida B. "The Detective's Report." *Richmond Planet*, October 14, 1899.

West, Elliott. *The Contested Plains: Indians, Goldseekers, and the Rush to Colorado*. Lawrence: University Press of Kansas, 1998.

Wexler, Sanford. *The Civil Rights Movement: An Eyewitness History*. New York: Facts on File, 1993.

White, Richard. "Trashing the Trails." In *Trails: Toward a New Western History*, edited by Patricia Nelson Limerick, Clyde A. Milner II, and Charles E. Rankin, 26–39. Lawrence: University Press of Kansas, 1991.

Whittington, Keith E. *Constitutional Interpretation: Textual Meaning, Original Intent, and Judicial Review*. Lawrence: University Press of Kansas, 1999.

Wiecek, William M. *The Sources of Antislavery Constitutionalism in America, 1760–1848*. Ithaca: Cornell University Press, 1977.

Williamson, Joel. *The Crucible of Race: Black/White Relations in the American South since Emancipation*. New York: Oxford University Press, 1984.

Wills, Garry. *A Necessary Evil: A History of American Distrust of Government*. New York: Simon and Schuster, 1999.

Wingrove, Elizabeth Rose. *Rousseau's Republican Romance*. Princeton: Princeton University Press, 2000.

Wolff, Robert Paul. "On Violence." *Journal of Philosophy* 66, no. 19, Sixty-Sixth Annual Meeting of the American Philosophical Association Eastern Division (1969): 601–16.

Wolin, Sheldon S. "Fugitive Democracy." In *Democracy and Difference: Contesting the Boundaries of the Political*, edited by Seyla Benhabib, 31–45. Princeton: Princeton University Press, 1996.

———. "Norm and Form: The Constitutionalizing of Democracy." In *Athenian Political Thought and the Reconstruction of American Democracy*, edited by J. Peter Euben, John R. Wallach, and Josiah Ober, 29–58. Ithaca: Cornell University Press, 1994.

———. *Politics and Vision: Continuity and Innovation in Western Political Thought*. Princeton: Princeton University Press, 2004.

Wood, Gordon S. *The Creation of the American Republic, 1776–1787*. Chapel Hill: University of North Carolina Press, 1998.

Wood, John A. *The Panthers and the Militias: Brothers under the Skin*? New York: University Press of America, 2002.

Woodward, C. Vann. *The Strange Career of Jim Crow*. New York: Oxford University Press, 1966.

———. *Tom Watson: Agrarian Rebel*. New York: Oxford University Press, 1987.

Wright, George C. *Racial Violence in Kentucky, 1865–1940: Lynchings, Mob Rule, and "Legal Lynchings."* Baton Rouge: Louisiana State University Press, 1990.

Wright, Henry C. "Ballot-Box and Battlefield." *Liberator*, March 25, 1842.

Wyatt-Brown, Bertram. "Prelude to Abolitionism: Sabbatarian Politics and the Rise of the Second Party System." *Journal of American History* 58, no. 2 (1971): 316–41.

———. *Southern Honor: Ethics and Behavior in the Old South*. New York: Oxford University Press, 1982.
Yates, William. *Rights of Colored Men to Suffrage, Citizenship, and Trial by Jury: Being a Book of Facts, Arguments and Authorities, Historical Notices and Sketches of Debates—with Notes*. Miami, FL: Mnemosyne Pub. Co., 1969.
Young, James P. *Reconsidering American Liberalism: The Troubled Odyssey of the Liberal Idea*. Boulder, CO: Westview Press, 1996.
Zangrando, Robert L. *The Naacp Crusade against Lynching, 1909–1950*. Philadelphia: Temple University Press, 1980.
Zerilli, Linda M. G. *Signifying Woman: Culture and Chaos in Rousseau, Burke, and Mill*. Ithaca, NY: Cornell University Press, 1994.
Zinn, Howard. *Disobedience and Democracy: Nine Fallacies on Law and Order*. New York: Random House, 1968.

INDEX